Hidden,
Not Forgotten

Discovering the Treasure of Unexpected Delays

Rebecca Sheffield

Scripture quotations in this book are taken from the Amplified Bible, unless otherwise noted in the text. Any emphasis in Scripture quotes is the author's own. The following Bible translations were used: King James Version (KJV), New King James Version (NKJ), copyright © 1979, 1980, 1982 by Thomas Nelson, Inc.

McDougal Publishing is a ministry of The McDougal Foundation, Inc., a Maryland nonprofit corporation dedicated to spreading the Gospel of the Lord Jesus Christ to as many people as possible in the shortest time possible.

Published by:
McDougal Publishing
P.O. Box 3595
Hagerstown, MD 21742-3595
www.mcdougalpublishing.com

ISBN 978-1-58158-088-4

Printed on demand in the U.S., the U.K. and Australia
For Worldwide Distribution

Contents

Dedication.. 4

Introduction.. 5

Preface 9

1. A Pocketful of Privacy 11
2. The Pathway to Promise...19
3. Weapon One: Let the Lord Define You.......................29
4. Weapon Two: Learn to Submit to Authority
   and to One Another..41
5. Weapon Three: Learn to Serve All People..................53
6. Weapon Four: Wait on the Lord
   to Reveal Your Identity 63
7. Weapon Five: Let the Lord Defend You 73
8. Weapon Six: Look to the Lord for
   Validation and Vindication 85
9. Weapon Seven: Let the Lord Reward
   Your Inheritance 97
10. Wrapped Up in the Glorious Rhythm...................... 109
11. Impossible to Miss..119

Dedication

This book is dedicated, first and foremost, to my heavenly Father. Only He and I know how many of the following pages were, in reality, penned by His hand and not mine.

I would also like to dedicate this work to my parents, Jasper and Jane Grier; not just because they are my parents, but because they chose to pass on to me two very special gifts. First, they passed on a desire to live in a way that is pleasing in the eyes of God. And second, they passed on a lifelong love for reading—anything and everything. Combined, these two gifts proved to be my inspiration and motivation to reach beyond my fears and attempt to do something "above and beyond all I could ask or think."

A special thanks to those who gave during this "process." You know who you are. You listened to me as I rambled on. You provided for me when I was in need. You supported me when the burden seemed too heavy. You helped me face new challenges with strength and courage. You are as much a part of this book as I am, and every life that is touched by reading it will be touched by you.

Introduction

All through the pages of history we read that God has chosen to use seasons of hiddenness to bring about His plan, purpose, and promise in the lives of His people. The Bible is full of instances in which God's chosen were tucked away by His design. They were set aside for a necessary time of testing and training in a concealed and private place. It is no different today. The Lord places you and me in pockets of preparation where He can reveal Himself and His ways *to* us, before He reveals Himself *through* us. You may be experiencing that place of hiding right now. "How can I tell?" you ask. "What does it look like?" Let me pose a few simple questions to you.

Do you find yourself trapped by the situations of life? Do you feel backed into a corner and incredibly uncomfortable? Do you view yourself as invisible behind all the stuff that surrounds you, constantly fighting for your attention? Does it seem as if you have lost yourself? Each day is the same as the one before, and you are asking, "How did I get here?"

Do you find yourself feeling forgotten by others, maybe even by God? The people you were close to seem to have other things going on that do not include you. Seemingly forgotten and set neatly folded high upon a shelf, you attempt to wait patiently and hope that this distance and isolation will soon pass. As the time crawls by, you are wondering, "Is this all there is?"

Do you find yourself questioning your identity and calling? You thought you knew who you were and what you were wired to do, but maybe you were mistaken. Other people's views of you differ from your own. Doubt has set up camp in your mind, it refuses eviction, and you are entertaining the thought, "Maybe I've missed it!"

Do you find yourself desperately wanting to believe in a God-ordained place for you? The Word says it has been designed and assigned (see Jeremiah 29:11; Ephesians 2:10).

Yet in spite of the dreams, visions, desires, and promises documented in His Word and written on your heart, nothing seems to be changing. You have not moved, and you are beginning to think, "I'm expecting too much!"

If you can identify with any of these descriptions, it may be that God is doing what He does best: getting your attention. How do I know? He got mine. Just like the prophet Habakkuk with regard to his disappointment and frustration...

You and I are watching for a sign.

> [Oh, I know I have been rash to talk out plainly this way to God!] *I will* [in my thinking] *stand upon my post of observation and station myself on the tower or fortress, and will watch to see what He will say within me and what answer I will make* [as His mouthpiece] *to the perplexities of my complaint against Him.*
>
> Habakkuk 2:1

You and I are waiting for things to change.

> *And the Lord answered me and said, Write the vision and engrave it plainly upon tablets that everyone who passes may* [be able to] *read* [it easily and quickly] *as he hastens by. For the vision is yet for an appointed time and it hastens to end* [fulfillment]; *it will not deceive or disappoint. Though it tarry, wait* [earnestly] *for it, because it will surely come; it will not be behindhand on its appointed day.* Habakkuk 2:2-3

You and I are becoming filled with faith in order for our God to fulfill His plans, purposes, and promises in us and through us.

> *Look at the proud; his soul is not straight or right within him, but the* [rigidly] *just and the* [uncompromisingly]

righteous man shall live by his faith and in his faithful-
ness. Habakkuk 2:4

If this is all true, then you and I are becoming people of faith, people of purpose, and people of promise. What can we learn during this season of discomfort, isolation, doubt, and questioning? What is it that the Lord would have us do as we watch for Him, wait on Him, and become more like Him? How do we take advantage of this precious time of being hidden alone with Him (see Psalm 27:5)?

I do not pretend to have all of the answers to these questions, but I do believe that you and I can benefit from one another's lessons learned during past trials, testing, and mistakes. We can turn them to our advantage. I have learned a few lessons along the way that I want to share with you solely for the purpose of bringing understanding, encouragement, and hope. But before we continue, dear friend, I want to clarify where I am coming from.

I am not a theologian, but one who has caught only a glimpse of understanding into a few of the many riches buried in the Word of God. I am not anyone of great significance, but one who gives value to the Kingdom of God only by doing her part; in other words, the only significance about me is the One who makes His home in me. I am not one easily provoked to wage war, but one who has recently acquired an overwhelming passion to join in an age-old battle for the sake of others. I do not sit in any position of honor by man's definition, but find myself tucked away in a hidden place by God's design. I am not one who has arrived, but one who continues on the journey set before her, still healing, still stumbling, and still growing.

Why grow? Why heal? Why continue the journey? Why run toward the goal, arrive, and complete the race (see 2 Timothy 4:7)? My friend, it is all for the glory of God and His Kingdom (see 1 Thessalonians 2:12). You and I each play a small but important role in history. We will be remembered for our contribution to it, both on this earth and in heaven.

We can choose to stay right where we are, isolated and frustrated, or we can submit to the life-changing power of God and allow Him to place us where and when He chooses. Yes, it will hurt, but it will also benefit. Yes, it means releasing the past, but it also means grabbing hold of the future. Yes, it will challenge us to our very core, but it will ultimately bring about fruit and fulfillment we never thought possible.

Now is the point of decision. You can put this book down and never pick it up again. You can lay it aside and read it later. Or, you can continue on and hopefully be enlightened, encouraged, and changed. Whatever your choice, be blessed my friend, as you continue your journey seeking truth and life. May you and I, together with all those that call upon the name of the Lord, attain oneness in faith, completeness of perfection, and the measure of the stature of the fullness of Christ (see Ephesians 4:12-13).

Preface

Promising Potential

This charge and admonition I commit in trust to you, Timothy, my son, in accordance with prophetic intimations which I formerly received concerning you, so that inspired and aided by them you may wage the good warfare. 1 Timothy 1:18

TWICE THE VISION, TWICE THE POWER

Rows and rows of soldiers stand at attention, extending far beyond what the natural eye can see. Each row is peculiarly narrow. The scene is broad and very general in nature, not allowing for the scrutiny of details such as age, gender, or even rank. Suddenly, the rear half of the army steps to the right in unison, and then forward to come alongside the front half. This tactical redistribution poses a much greater threat to the enemy than anyone involved could have foreseen. As a result, the front lines double in size, allowing twice the vision and twice the show of power.

THE WORKERS ARE FEW

Currently, the Army of God is not operating at its full potential. A faithful few carry out the work of many. How is that possible? There are those who are young in the faith and undergoing recovery, healing, and training in the basics of the Christian life. They are not yet ready for battle. There are those who have been holding themselves back out of laziness and fear. They are not yet willing to battle. There are those who have been held back by others, for whatever reason. They have not been permitted to battle. Naturally, none of this comes as a surprise to our Commander in Chief, King Jesus.

His vision for His Army has always been for it to be walking in fullness, unity, and victory (see Ephesians 1:22-23;

4:1-3; 6:10-11). Under His direction and by His hand, many more will be mobilized very soon. Those who have been in training will be made ready, those who have been holding back will step forward, and those who have been held back will be released. But before this can occur, those who have been on the front lines must determine to receive willingly those who are coming forward suddenly.

I share this bird's-eye view of the Lord's Army with you in order to communicate the soberness of the times and the need for unity like never before. Each soldier must be strategically placed in order for the promise of victory to be fulfilled. The victory I speak of is the victory over the plan of the enemy to destroy the harvest of souls that will soon cover the earth (see John 10:10). With this harvest in mind, the following pages have been dedicated to assist those who discover themselves currently hidden, standing near the rear of the Army of God, recognizing that soon they will be called upon to step up, to step out, and to fight.

CHAPTER ONE

A Pocketful of Privacy

*He who dwells in the secret place of the Most High
shall remain stable and fixed under the shadow of the
Almighty* [Whose power no foe can withstand].
Psalm 91:1

Have you ever played the word association game? It is the one where I say a word, and you say the first thing that comes to mind. For example, if I say the word *hidden*, what do you think of first? Maybe it is a family secret, passed down from generation to generation, concealed from all outsiders. Or it could be a delicate matter of the heart, deeply desired and longed for, yet lingering on the edge of out of sight. It might be a beautiful work of art waiting to be revealed and admired, but veiled by a dividing cloth. Maybe what you think of first is a treasure buried in an unknown location deep beneath the sand which will remain untouched until you discover it with shovel in hand. If your reply is anything remotely similar to these examples, you probably have some understanding of what it means to be hidden.

To be *hidden* is to be "concealed, out of sight, veiled, or buried."[1] In order for something to be revealed, it must first be hidden. Hiddenness precedes revelation. The Lord has chosen it to be so (see Deuteronomy 29:29; Amos 3:7). And though seasons of being concealed and out of sight can prove to be very lonely, painful, and frustrating, they can also yield intimacy, liberty, and an understanding that produces eternal results. The Bible is full of illustrations of ordinary people who were divinely led into a period of hiding, only to be exposed in the fullness of time to bring about significant outcomes.

HIDDEN BIRTH (EXODUS, CHAPTERS 2-12)

Moses experienced hiding at almost every stage of his life. In order to protect him from being abducted and drowned in the river Nile, he was hidden at birth (see Exodus 2:1-4). For three months his mother concealed him, veiled in a blanket, surrounded by the four walls of his home. At the age of three months, Moses was tucked away in a basket and placed in the rushes on the edge of the same river previously determined to be his tomb. Exposure came, met with compassion, and we find Moses surrounded by another set of walls, only this time in the shape of an Egyptian palace (see Exodus 2:5-10). This palace would become his home. It would be a place of protection. It would be a place of provision.

As time passed, Moses grew into a man of vast wealth and extreme power. But the pull of power and possessions was no match for his God-given purpose and the cries of his enslaved people. Eventually, the palace walls that had faithfully provided and protected could no longer hold him inside. Through a chain of events, at the age of forty, Moses was forced to flee the palace walls seeking sanctuary from the wrath of Pharaoh and found himself hidden once again (see Exodus 2:11-15). Only this time he was hidden in exile. As he made camp in Midian, Moses discovered not only family, but also freedom. For forty years he tended sheep and enjoyed a life of liberty and love. All the while, the Lord used this time to prepare Moses for the work He had planned for him. By the time he approached his second experience with exposure, Moses had learned a great deal. He learned how to be a submissive son to Jethro, a dedicated husband to Zipporah, a loving father for Gershom, a compassionate shepherd to the sheep, and a devoted follower of the great I AM (see Exodus 2:16–3:14).

Hidden at birth, hidden in a palace, hidden in exile, Moses was sent back to Egypt at the command of the God of Abraham, Isaac, and Jacob. Called to be God's messenger, ruler, deliverer, and redeemer, Moses found that his authority was not recognized by his own people. The call of Moses was hidden from the sight of man until the Lord chose to reveal it through many miraculous signs and wonders. Yet in spite of all that the Lord had done to reveal His chosen leader, His people continued to question Him and His choice at every turn (see Exodus 3:2–12:51).

Moses was an ordinary man who found himself in the middle of God's plan to deliver His people from bondage. Unaware of God's plan during the hidden times of his life, he did the best he could with what he had, and God did the rest. Moses was hidden at birth, hidden in a palace, hidden in exile, hidden in calling, lived through it all, and made a difference.

HIDDEN HERITAGE (THE BOOK OF ESTHER)

Esther also found herself living inside palace walls. A beautiful, young, Jewish virgin captured by the king's men, Esther found herself hidden in the midst of a harem. Selected as a possible queen for a king who had discarded his first wife because of his displeasure with her, Esther was charged by her guardian Mordecai to conceal her unfavorable nationality (see Esther 2:5-10).

With her heritage hidden and her new home a harem, Esther discovered that her revised daily routine for the next twelve months would be one of beauty treatments: six months with oil of myrrh, and six months with sweet spices and perfumes. Finally, at the end of one year, Esther was presented to the king for inspection and was chosen as the most favored of all the candidates (see Esther 2:12-18).

When the time came for Esther to be challenged concerning her heritage and her devotion to her people, she was prepared to stand strong and act as God's mouthpiece. And in the face of possible death and destruction for all the Jews, her voice was heard, her request was honored, and her people were given the opportunity to fight for themselves with dignity and strength (see Esther 3:1-9:32).

Esther, through no choice of her own, was placed in a position of great influence and great honor, even though it seemed like prison at the time. By submitting herself to God's chosen authority, she invited Him to use her to bring about a pivotal change in the history of His beloved people. Esther, much like Moses, made herself available and made a difference.

HIDDEN IDENTITY (GENESIS, CHAPTERS 37-50)

Joseph's encounters with hiddenness did not include the luxury of palace walls until after several stopovers in prison. His first experience found him hidden in the bottom of an empty well into which his angry, jealous brothers had violently tossed him after stripping him of his coat. Unable to finish what they had begun, they sold him to a caravan of slave traders passing by on their way to Egypt. In one day, Joseph had gone from favored son to fettered slave by the hands of those who should have protected him (see Genesis 37:1-36).

When brotherly affection was found lacking, heavenly protection came in and made the difference. At the hand of God, Joseph rose to the top, becoming the trusted assistant to Potiphar, the captain and chief executioner of Pharaoh's royal guard (see Genesis 39:1-6). Then anger and pride waged war against righteousness in an attempt to lead Joseph astray. Unwilling to turn his back on his God, Joseph refused the immoral offer, was accused of insult, and was cast into prison at the accusations of Potiphar's malicious wife (see Genesis 39:7-20). But once again God's hand moved, and Joseph was promoted (see Genesis 39:21-23).

Tossed into and hidden in a well, sold into slavery and seemingly forgotten by his brothers, accused and hidden in jail and temporarily forgotten by his cell mate, Joseph used every opportunity to forgive and move forward, no matter where the starting line fell. With each new challenge, God was showing Joseph that he could make a difference wherever he found himself. In this truth, he became not only a faithful servant, but also an empowered leader.

After being called upon to interpret Pharaoh's dream and being found *"intelligent and discreet and understanding and wise,"* (Genesis 41:39) Joseph was recognized as *"a man in whom is the spirit of God"* by Pharaoh himself (Genesis 41:38). He was immediately elevated to second in command of all of Egypt. While faithfully executing the duties entrusted to him, Joseph eventually met with his brothers face-to-face. The encounter was an emotional one. Unable to reveal his identity, Joseph decided to test his brothers to see if they had come to a position of regret and repentance where he was concerned. After several encounters, He was led to reveal his true identity to his brothers alone in a closed room. The family was reunited and received into the land of Egypt where they prospered and multiplied during Pharaoh's reign (see Genesis 42:6-47:27).

Joseph, cast aside by family, found himself hidden by God's design. He realized that he had been sent ahead, and that all he had endured was not only for the good of Egypt and its people, but also for the good of his family. He spoke to them lovingly, explaining that all this had taken place *"to preserve for you a posterity and to continue a remnant on the earth and to save your lives by a great escape and save for you many survivors"* (Genesis 45:7). Joseph made the most of every opportunity, and in doing so he honored his God. His appropriate reactions to the dark, lonely hidden places of life and his ability to consider wherever he found himself as home opened the door for the salvation and preservation of his people.

Hidden Heart (Luke 1:26–2:51)

Finding its home in her heart, Mary's form of hiddenness was the most difficult of all to detect. Her story began with a private visitation from an angel announcing that she would become pregnant with a very special child (see Luke 1:26-38). This pregnancy would not come about in the usual way, but would occur through the power of the Spirit of the living God. Meeting with unfavorable reaction from those around her, including her beloved Joseph, Mary discovered herself caught between God's ability and man's inability. For God was able to bypass nature and create a new life in a new way, but man was unable to comprehend it.

The time arrived for a hidden delivery within months of the miraculous conception. Mary and Joseph had traveled far to report to their place of origin, adhering to the decree for a census to be taken (see Luke 2:1-5). The young expectant couple found themselves in an animal stall delivering their long anticipated yet highly controversial child (see Luke 2:6-7). Not long after the birth, strangers came to admire the newborn baby. To the joy of all present, along with the visit of admiration came words of declaration. Those words, spoken by simple shepherds that day, found their sanctuary in Mary's heart for many years to come (see Luke 2:17-19).

Not long after His arrival, the infant was taken to the Temple to be dedicated (see Luke 2:22-24). At the Temple that day, this new life on earth intersected with another life that was about to end. Although unable to see the child, the blind Simeon was overwhelmed with joy. He detected by the Spirit that he was in the presence of the Messiah, the Anointed One promised by God (see Luke 2:25-27). He, like the shepherds before him, came with words of declaration (see Luke 2:28-35), and they too found a hiding place, closely and persistently guarded in Mary's heart (see Luke 2:33).

Twelve years later, young Jesus was found ministering in the Temple after a frantic search for Him by His parents (see Luke 2:41-50). From His own lips came His simple yet profound explanation that they should have known He would be in His Father's house, going about His Father's business (see Luke 2:49). Though Mary could not intellectually understand what her son was saying, she did what any mother would do; she took it to heart (see Luke 2:50-51).

Mary alone carried the truth concerning the child she bore, the boy she nurtured, and the man she followed. She carried that truth from the day He was born, to the day He died, to the day He rose again. To reveal the hidden treasure prematurely would have been pointless. Who would have listened? Who would have believed? Mary chose to make a difference by allowing God to use her as a treasure chest devoted to carrying the greatest treasures of all: first, the treasured body of the babe in her womb; second, the treasured future of the man in her heart.

In each account we have discovered that it was God who made the decision to conceal His plan for His people, for the sake of His glory and for the sake of His Kingdom. While they were hidden in His divine pocket of privacy in birth, in heritage, in identity, even in heart, they were at no time forgotten by Him. To be *forgotten* is to be "overlooked, considered gone, ancient history, out of sight and out of mind."[2] Moses was not forgotten, but prepared. Esther was not forgotten, but purified. Joseph was not forgotten, but promoted. Mary was not forgotten, but proved.

You and I have been called into this same plan of God's, for the sake of His Kingdom and the sake of His glory. We now find ourselves in great company and can be assured that the God who trained and sustained these precious people will do the same for us. He will place His hand of grace upon us (see Psalm 139:5) and reveal the hidden places in His perfect time (see Daniel 2:22), in a way that we could never anticipate. As we wait on Him, we must rely on Him to temper us, train us, and work His character in us (see Philippians 2:13).

We have taken the time to select and view snapshots of just a few of the many instances in the Bible where God's people experienced times of *hiddenness*. There are many more we could expound on, each one possessing its own uniqueness. To do so would take volumes. But let's flip through the pages of one more photo album. This album tells the story of an ordinary woman living in extraordinary times. She too was watching for a sign, waiting for things to change, and becoming a person of faith. In the midst of all her disappointment, confusion, and despair, God was able to impart a maturity and wisdom that would become her greatest strength. This strength would prove to be her unconscious invitation for the empowerment of God to produce His promise in her and through her. He gave her a new hope. He gave her a new name: Sarah (see Genesis 17:15-16).

DISCUSSION QUESTIONS

1. I consider myself as one who is...
   a. Young in the faith and not yet ready for battle.
   b. Holding back and not yet willing to battle.
   c. Held back and not yet permitted to battle.

Explain.

2. When I hear the word *hidden*, I immediately think of...

3. I can identify with the story of...
   a. The hidden birth of Moses.
   b. The hidden heritage of Esther.
   c. The hidden identity of Joseph.
   d The hidden heart of Mary.

Explain.

4. I admit that I am (ready/not ready) to step up and step out to fight.

Explain.

CHAPTER TWO

The Pathway to Promise

He leads the humble in what is right, and the humble He teaches His way.   Psalm 25:9

THE WALLS WE BUILD

The lives of Abraham and Sarah have been the focus of my studies for several years. This study has not been one of great theological effort but has leaned more toward practical application. During my investigation of and fascination with this patriarchal couple, I found myself puzzled and sometimes frustrated by a few of the choices they made. Recognizing that these choices were made during times of duress brought no relief.

The frustration began with Abraham when he so easily dispensed with his wife the minute things got tough, and then it grew with Sarah and her total devotion and cooperation throughout the whole ordeal. It was puzzling to me how anyone would place someone so dear in such a precarious position, and even more puzzling to me why anyone would agree to such a thing. But before we continue, let us take a moment to review what led up to the choices to which I am referring.

Abram and Sarai are first introduced in chapter eleven of the book of Genesis. In that introduction, we are given several details that will prove to be very significant as we further investigate this portion of scripture. The first key is that Abram and Sarai were husband and wife (see Genesis 11:29). The second key we learn is that Sarai was barren, a woman without children (see Genesis 11:30). To be *barren* is to be "unproductive, unfruitful, empty, and incapable of bringing about results."[3] The third key we discover is that Abram's father, Terah, decided to pack up all of their belongings and travel from Ur to the land of Canaan (see Genesis 11:31). For some unknown reason, the traveling family never reached the land of Canaan under his leadership, but stopped and settled in Haran instead.

It was there in Haran that Terah died (see Genesis 11:32), and it was also there that the Lord first spoke to Abram (see Genesis 12:1-3). His instructions were simply to finish what his father had begun; he was to leave his country, his relatives, and his father's house, and travel to the land of Canaan. Along with these instructions came three promises: the promise of becoming a great nation, the promise of increase, and the promise of fame. Abram obediently packed up his household and departed Haran as the Lord commanded, taking Sarai and his nephew Lot along with him. Reaching his destination, actually passing through it, Abram pitched his tent between Bethel and Ai and immediately built an altar to the Lord (see Genesis 12:4-8).

An unforeseen famine came upon the land. In order to escape starvation and devastation, Abram led his family to Egypt, believing it to be a temporary solution to the immediate threat. It was in Egypt that Abram and Sarai made a decision that would literally establish a wall between them, placing Sarai in a position of extreme danger and potential moral ruin.

And when he [Abram] *was about to enter into Egypt, he said to Sarai his wife, I know that you are beautiful to behold. So when the Egyptians see you, they will say, This is his wife; and they will kill me, but they will let you live. Say, I beg of you, that you are my sister, so that it may go well with me for your sake and my life will be spared because of you. And when Abram came into Egypt, the Egyptians saw that the woman was very beautiful. The princes of Pharaoh also saw her and commended her to Pharaoh, and she was taken into Pharaoh's house* [harem]. *And he treated Abram well for her sake; he acquired sheep, oxen, he-donkeys, menservants, maidservants, she-donkeys, and camels. But the Lord scourged Pharaoh and his household with serious plagues because of Sarai, Abram's wife. And Pharaoh called Abram and said, What is this that you have done to me? Why did you not tell me that she was your wife? Why did you say, She is my sister, so that I took her to be my wife? Now then, here is your wife; take her and get away* [from here]*! And Pharaoh commanded his men concerning him, and they brought him on his way with his wife and all that he had.*

Genesis 12:11-20

Abram and Sarai agreed to broadcast a falsehood concerning their relationship. The reason behind it was purely and simply survival. Abram requested of Sarai to say she was his sister, believing that this would keep them both alive. Sarai complied and found herself immediately confiscated, presented to Pharaoh, and added to his collection of women. As a result of her own actions, she had become a lady in waiting: waiting to be rescued, waiting to be defiled. We do not know how many days, weeks, or months she spent hidden in that palace, but it must have seemed like an eternity to her.

Can you imagine the thoughts that must have tormented her mind? "What have we done? This can't really be happening! I can't possibly stay here! I'm another man's wife! I made a mistake, a big mistake, but how do I fix it? I can't fix it, not without making things worse! What am I going to do? Nothing. I'll do nothing. I'll leave that to Abram. He'll come for me. He'll find a way to get me out of here. He will, won't he? What if he can't? What am I supposed to do when Pharaoh actually summons me? I can't even think about that right now! Oh, my God, what have we done?"

Once the scheme devised by Abram and Sarai was uncovered and Sarai's true identity was exposed as the wife and half sister of Abram, Pharaoh sent them packing. They found themselves right back where they started, pitching their tent in between Bethel and Ai (see Genesis 13:3-4). Although Abram and Sarai slipped out of God's plan, in

His loving patience He waited for them to complete the process and then led them back to where they were before the blunder began.

In chapter fifteen of Genesis we find Abram experiencing an encounter with God. This encounter came to him in the form of a vision, a word picture if you will. In this vision the Lord unveiled and released an additional detail in His plan: Abram was to beget an heir. This heir would be the one who would inherit all Abram possessed, including not only material wealth, but also the promised blessings previously pronounced by God (see Genesis 15:1-5).

Time passed, and we read in chapter sixteen that Sarai, in her impatience, decided that the promise of an heir was not being fulfilled soon enough. So she took it upon herself to provide a way for an heir to be given to her husband through the womb of her handmaiden. Abram conceded. The maid was provided and a child was born and given the name Ishmael.

When Abram reached the age of ninety-nine, God's promise of an heir was once again repeated to him in even greater detail (see Genesis 17:1-22). This detailed unfolding of God's plan, once and for all, established the fact that Abram's firstborn son, Ishmael, was not the child that God had originally promised. Yes, he was his son, but there would be another, and Sarai would be the one to carry and deliver him. Abram and Sarai were not only told to antici-pate a new addition to their family, they were also told that they were to accept their new names, Abraham and Sarah. Why the new names? It pleased the Lord to do so, and it would ultimately bring Him glory. He was about to do a new thing in and through these two people that would have eternal results. In order to establish His plan and purpose as the one propelling force in their daily lives, He gave them each a new name and a new cause. They were to see themselves as the father and mother of many nations (see Genesis 17:4, 16).

You and I know that accepting what is given to us from the Lord is one thing, but living it out day-to-day is quite another. History and experience both tell us that returning to old habits takes much less faith and effort than establishing new ones. It was no different for the father-to-be and the mother-to-be. And once again, in chapter twenty, we find Abraham and Sarah returning to their old ways.

Now Abraham journeyed from there toward the South country (the Negeb) and dwelt between Kadesh and Shur; and he lived temporarily in Gerar. And Abraham said of Sarah his wife, She is my sister. And Abimelech king of Gerar sent and took Sarah [into his harem]. *But God came to Abimelech in a dream by night and said, Behold, you are a dead man because of the woman you have taken* [as your own], *for she is a man's wife. But Abimelech had not come near her, so he said, Lord, will you slay a people who are just and innocent? Did not the man tell me, She is my sister? And she herself said, He is my brother. In integrity of heart and innocency of hands I have done this. Then God said to him in the dream, Yes, I know you did this in the integrity of your heart, for it was I Who kept you back and spared you from sinning against Me; therefore I did not give you occasion to touch her. So now restore to the man his wife, for he is a prophet, and he will pray for you and you will live. But if you do not restore her* [to him], *know that you shall surely die, you and all who are yours. So Abimelech rose early in the morning and called all his servants and told them all these things; and the men were exceedingly filled with reverence and fear. Then Abimelech called Abraham and said to him, What have you done to us? And how have I offended you that you have brought on me and my kingdom a great sin? You have done to me what ought not to be done* [to anyone]. *And Abimelech said to Abraham, What did you see* [in us] *that* [justified] *you in doing such a thing as this? And Abraham said, Because I thought, Surely there is no reverence or fear of God at all in this place,*

23

and they will slay me because of my wife. But truly, she is my sister; she is the daughter of my father but not of my mother; and she became my wife. When God caused me to wander from my father's house, I said to her, This kindness you can show me: at every place we stop, say of me, he is my brother. Then Abimelech took sheep and oxen and male and female slaves and gave them to Abraham and restored to him Sarah his wife. And Abimelech said, Behold, my land is before you: dwell wherever it pleases you. And to Sarah he said, Behold, I have given to this brother of yours a thousand pieces of silver; see, it is to compensate you [for all that has occurred] *and to vindicate your honor before all who are with you; before all men you are cleared and compensated.*

Genesis 20:1-16

I have read this passage over and over again, trying to make some sense out of what both Abraham and Sarah attempted to do, not just once, but twice! And I admit to you that I do not know what I would have done if I had found myself in the same circumstances; therefore I cannot declare myself judge and bring down a sentence upon them. But there is something I can do, and that is to admit that after much thought and many question-and-answer sessions with the Lord, I have come to a conclusion concerning Abraham and Sarah. I have concluded that it would be more to my advantage to overlook how they got themselves into such a jam, and pay more attention to how they handled themselves in the middle of it. But before we look at the "how" of this account, let us ask the question "what?" What was it about Abraham and Sarah and their situation that is comparable to the condition of the Lord's Army described earlier?

WEAPONS OF CHOICE

The previous accounts of Abraham and Sarah and the condition of the Lord's Army share several things in common. First, each account includes a God-sized promise. Abraham and Sarah had the promise of a child when it was humanly impossible for such a thing to happen (see Genesis 17:15-17). The Lord's Army has His promise of victory over the plans of the enemy (see 1 John 5:4-5), resulting in a great harvest (see Revelation 7:9-10), in a time when great darkness and perversion have a hold on much of the world. Second, each account requires that all parties concerned must be involved in order for the promise to be fulfilled. Abraham could not conceive a child on his own and neither could Sarah. Physical separation meant temporary fruitlessness. It took both of them working together before the child could be conceived (see Genesis 21:1-3). In order for the promise of victory in the Lord's Army to be realized, all those who have signed up must be present, accounted for, and cooperating. Existing in such an environment of unity would bring about the Lord's anointing, power, and strength so that His purposes could be fulfilled (see Psalm 133:1-3). Third, each account reveals a struggle with dysfunction. Out of fear and immaturity, yet pregnant with potential, Abraham and Sarah made a mistake and held back information, which resulted in a painful delay (see Genesis 12:11-20, 20:1-16). Out of fear and immaturity, yet called to conquer, the Lord's Army has also made mistakes. These have led it down a path of disunity, rendering it unable to bring about the desired result: effectiveness for the Kingdom.

What became of Abraham and Sarah? Yes, they were hidden from one another for a time. Yes, it was a time of insecurity and doubt. Yes, the promise was delayed for a season, but it came as no surprise to the One who first spoke the promise (see Psalm 139:16). It was in those dark times of separation, doubt, and dysfunction that the Lord worked His purposes into Abraham and Sarah, propelling each of them separately to a deeper level of strength, maturity, and reliance upon their God. Then, at His hand, and in His timing, they were joined together once again and the promise of an heir was eventually fulfilled.

What will become of the Army of the Lord? Yes, there are those who have been hidden for a time. Yes, it is a time of insecurity and doubt. Yes, the promise of victory has been delayed for a season, but it comes as no surprise to the One who first spoke it. In this time of isolation, He is working in us, propelling each of us to a deeper level of strength, maturity, and reliance upon Him (see Philippians 2:1). Then, at His hand, and in His time, His army will unite in power and His promise will be fulfilled.

The written account of Abraham and Sarah is a gift to us. And when we allow ourselves to be instructed, enlightened, and encouraged by what is revealed in it, then we will be able to take hold of the subtle yet powerful weapons that have been made available to the Army of the Lord through it. As we focus on Sarah in her time of hiddenness, we will be able to pinpoint what it was that ultimately prepared her to walk respectfully alongside her husband and become the mother of nations she was destined to be (see Genesis 17:16).

Sarah chose her weapons well. She did not make use of the weapons that so easily come to mind, such as bows and arrows, sticks and stones, or intimidation and manipulation. Sarah's weapons of choice were much more powerful and much more reliable; they were the weapons of humility. It was her attitude toward her circumstances and the people responsible for her very life that brought Sarah through her darkest hours. In her confusion, she let the Lord define who she was and what she was called to do. In her captivity, she learned how to submit to those in authority over her. In her confinement, she learned how to serve all people with kindness. In her time of concealment, she waited on the Lord to reveal her true identity to all. In her weakness, she let the Lord defend her. In her worthlessness, she looked to the Lord for validation. In her humiliation, she looked to the Lord for vindication. In her moments of hopelessness and lack, she let the Lord provide.

These weapons threaten to defy all of our modern thinking. We have been taught that we have rights. We must speak up for ourselves. We must use every weapon at our disposal. We must do whatever it takes to secure our dignity and our position in life. To a small degree these statements are true; we are not to be doormats or to be used by anyone who is stronger, but there is also a time when these statements do not ring true. That is the time when humility is our only resource, our only strength. It is the time when our hands are tied, our weapons prove ineffective, and we recognize that our only hope is of a divine nature.

What will you and I do in our hours of darkness? What will we do when doubt and confusion haunt us? How will we handle ourselves when we recognize we are weak and defenseless? What weapons will we take up and use when we are backed into a corner? Who will you and I turn to when we feel worthless and hopeless? Hopefully, we will follow Sarah's lead and learn to walk humbly with our God (see Micah 6:8). "Where do I start?" you ask. "What will it take?" You start by becoming familiar with the first weapon of humility, which is identifying with the Lord and letting Him define who you are.

DISCUSSION QUESTIONS

1. Have you ever made a choice that put another person in possible danger? Explain.

2. Have you ever agreed to be placed in a dangerous situation at the request of another? Explain.

3. How easy would it be to return to a bad habit after resolving to change? Can you think of an example?

4. Is it a challenge for you to keep from judging others when they make mistakes? Why?

5. Is there a wall that separates you and someone you love that requires dismantling? What could you do to begin the process?

6. What main truth have you gathered from this account of Abraham and Sarah that might be of value to you in the future?

7. Can you describe a time in your life when your hands were tied and your only hope was of a divine nature?

8. Define *humility* in one word.

CHAPTER THREE

Weapon One: Let the Lord Define You

For in Him we live and move and have our being…
For we are also His offspring.   Acts 17:28

WHAT LIES BENEATH

Picture yourself sitting in the middle of a warm, comfy room with several of your closest friends. Suddenly, the discussion turns from your opinion of the latest hit movie to those serious and agonizing questions about your purpose in life. Your hands begin to sweat. Your stomach converts into a habitat for butterflies. You have no other choice but to kick into your "invisible mode," avoiding all eye contact, erasing any expression from your face, and breathing shallowly to ensure that a heavy sigh is not mistaken for that breath we take right before we have something to say. You are reminded of how uncomfortable you become when people ask these kinds of questions. Why is that? Why does this have to be so difficult for you? As you continue to fret, someone in the room begins to speak, permitting you to breathe a sigh of relief. As you listen to what they have to say, you think to yourself, "Wow, they really have it all together," so much so that it makes you want to lash out irrationally!

The good news is that you are not alone. There are many of us who are still in the process of discovering who we are and what we were wired to do. Granted, we know our names, and most of us know where we came from. We each have a general idea of what our tendencies and talents might be. We know what we like, and we certainly know what we don't like. But something seems to be missing, something that can't be described.

Let me ask you, is there the slightest possibility that there is nothing missing at all? Could it be that what seems to be missing is actually hidden just below the surface, patiently waiting to be released? Could it be that what we know about ourselves is only a small portion of what is yet to come, the beginning of what is yet to be revealed? There is still so much to discover and it will take a lifetime to complete such a task, but that is no reason to delay getting started. We can take what we currently know and allow God to begin forming a true picture for us. Then as new insights surface, they can be added one by one.

To start, you and I must be willing to take a good, long look in the mirror and permit God to examine us and establish truths about us that we were never willing to see before. More often than not, we spend a good portion of our time only scratching the surface, neglecting to dig deeper in order to discover the hidden treasures inside. We have all experienced the tendency to take the less intrusive method by attempting to form our own definitions of ourselves using outward appearances: our clothing preferences, our trendy hairstyles, and our physical abilities. We invest in all types of personality tests in order to apply labels to those things about us that seem to come so naturally: introvert or extrovert, feeler or thinker, internal processor or external processor. We might also take the time to look at our credentials, roles, careers, hobbies, and creative expressions, allowing them to define who we are. My friend, though all of these things have a valid place in our lives, it will take more than a new hairstyle, a label, a degree, and a knack for sports to define you and me. It will take an honest look at the things that lie deep within.

It is on the inside, in the deeper places, we encounter the heart, the hope, and the home of our real selves. A face-to-face meeting with the things that motivate our emotions, thoughts, and actions is an encounter with the heart. How we will feel, what we will think, and what we will do in any situation is determined there. Where the heart is the motivation, hope is the expectation. Recognizing who or what we have entrusted our future to undoubtedly defines our source of hope. And it is that source of hope that molds and shapes our expectations. What we expect and our attitude about life depend on where our hope lies. If the heart reveals motivation and hope reveals expectation, then it is the home that reveals destination. Wherever we feel most at home is where we are destined to spend eternity, unless we make a decision to change. Home is the place we have set as our goal. It is our intended settling place. It is what we long for, whether consciously or unconsciously. It is the ultimate propeller of life and the finishing line that lies ahead of each one of us. Understanding our heart motives, realizing where our hope lies, and recognizing our destination home are all necessary encounters with what is buried on the inside.

When we speak of defining ourselves, we are actually talking about identity. Identity defines who or what we are. It allows each of us to be individual and unique and provides us with a true sense of self. Identity defines our character as good or bad, strong or weak, and reveals our personality, those traits that make us different from everyone else. It is who or what we connect ourselves to that determines a large portion of our identity. The things and the people that we have connected with define more about us than anything else. When we choose to be affiliated with a person, a cause, a religion, we are saying that we stand for what they stand for, that we are in agreement. Therefore, the company you keep and the causes that you support contribute greatly to defining your character. Ask yourself, "What have I attached myself to? With whom do I identify?" The answers to these questions may be difficult to admit. They have been for me. But keep in mind that recognizing who you are today and what you have been bound to in the past does not have to affect you for the rest of your life. Each new day grants a fresh opportunity to release the unwanted chains of the past and take hold of the new possibilities of the future. To take advantage of this opportunity, you will have to change some areas of your life. Although those changes will require effort and determination, they will bring about eternal results.

Why would anyone want to change their current identity? Why can't things just stay the way they are? Why make such a big deal about it? We seek change because how we live our lives is determined by our identity. It is our fingerprint for life, our legacy to others, and our contribution to this world. It governs our decisions. It shapes what we will impart to others. It outlines what will be remembered about us after we are gone. Why change? We change because there is not one of us who has arrived. We change because others are watching us, following us, and relying on us. We change because we want our time on this earth to amount to something more than just living out our appointed days. We change because we want to make a difference, and in order to do so, things cannot stay the way they are. We cannot stay the way we are.

To change or build upon our current self-identity requires an understanding of how identity is developed. Three independent sources, each impressive, important, and influential, contribute to the intricate formation of identity. The first involves how we relate to ourselves. The second stems from our relationships with other people. The third, and most powerful, concerns our relationship with God.

Who do I say that I am?

It is no secret that you and I have the ability to talk ourselves into, or out of, just about anything. And this capability we possess can be used to our advantage or to our disadvantage. We can engage it to encourage and build ourselves up, or we can empower it to discourage and tear ourselves down. We can choose to treat ourselves with love and respect, or we can choose to misuse and abuse ourselves with no self-respect at all. We can lie to ourselves and say that we are unimportant, useless, unwanted and unloved; or we can accept the truth. Where does this truth come from? It comes from a source that always encourages, always loves, and always respects. Who is that source? It is Father God.

Who do they say that I am?

How others talk about us, act around us, and try to label us can also make quite an impact on how we see ourselves. Many studies have proven that a child's early years and the relationships formed during them play a vital role in how they view themselves. It would be helpful for us to know which beliefs about ourselves were adopted from the ideas of others, determine the truth of these beliefs, and then throw out the lies.

Let me explain. The people we love and respect speak words to us and about us that express either love or hate. Actions and reactions are directed toward us that come from either a healthy heart or a broken heart. Good labels and bad labels are attached to us that originate from either a desire to encourage or a desire to discourage. All of these have contributed to our sense of self. Because of this, you and I must learn how to filter every word, every action and reaction, and every label that comes from those around us by testing them against the truth. Where does this truth come from? It comes from a source that always expresses love, always deals with us from a pure heart, and always desires to encourage us. Who is that source? It is Father God.

Who does God say that I am?

We can choose to rely on our own definition of self, hoping that what we have decided upon is an honest and true evaluation. We can choose to rely on how others attempt to define us, believing that what they are able to see is accurate and what they know is best. Or, we can rely on Father God's definition of us, trusting in His love for us, leaning on His understanding about us, and believing in His plan for us. His words spoken over us always bring life. His actions toward us always show love. His description of us always brings hope. The words of our heavenly Father paraphrased in the "Father's Love Letter" say it best:

FATHER'S LOVE LETTER

*You may not know me, but I know everything about you…*Psalm 139:1

I know when you sit down and when you rise up… Psalm 139:2

*I am familiar with all your ways…*Psalm 139:3

Even the very hairs on your head are numbered… Matthew 10:29-31

*For you were made in My image…*Genesis 1:27

*In Me you live and move and have your being…*Acts 17:28

*For you are My offspring…*Acts 17:28

*I knew you even before you were conceived…*Jeremiah 1:4-5

*I chose you when I planned creation…*Ephesians 1:11-12

*You were not a mistake…*Psalm 139:15-16

*For all your days are written in My book…*Psalm 139:15-16

*I determined the exact time of your birth and where you would live…*Acts 17:26

*You are fearfully and wonderfully made…*Psalm 139:14

*I knit you together in your mother's womb…*Psalm 139:13

And brought you forth on the day you were born… Psalm 71:6

*I have been misrepresented by those who don't know Me…*John 8:41-44

*I am not distant and angry, but am the complete expression of love…*1 John 4:16

*And it is My desire to lavish My love on you…*1 John 3:1

*Simply because you are My child and I am your Father…*1 John 3:1

*I offer more than your earthly father ever could…*Matthew 7:11

*For I am the perfect Father…*Matthew 5:48

Every good gift that you receive comes from My hand…
James 1:17

For I am your provider and I meet all your needs…
Matthew 6:31-33

*My plan for your future has always been filled with hope…*Jeremiah 29:11

*Because I love you with an everlasting love…*Jeremiah 31:3

*My thoughts toward you are countless as the sand on the seashore…*Psalm 139:17-18

*And I rejoice over you with singing…*Zephaniah 3:17

*I will never stop doing good to you…*Jeremiah 32:40

*For you are My treasured possession…*Exodus 19:5

*I desire to establish you with all My heart and all My soul…*Jeremiah 32:41

And I want to show you great and marvelous things…
Jeremiah 33:3

If you seek me with all your heart, you will find Me…
Deuteronomy 4:29

*Delight in Me and I will give you the desires of your heart…*Psalm 37:4

*For it is I who gave you those desires…*Philippians 2:13

*I am able to do more for you than you could possibly imagine…*Ephesians 3:20

*For I am your greatest encourager…*2 Thessalonians 2:16-17

*I am also the Father who comforts you in all your troubles…*2 Corinthians 1:3-4

*When you are brokenhearted, I am close to you…*Psalm 34:18

*As a shepherd carries a lamb, I have carried you close to My heart…*Isaiah 40:11

One day I will wipe away every tear from your eyes…
Revelation 21:3-4

*And I'll take away all the pain you have suffered on this earth…*Revelation 21:4

*I am your Father and I love you even as I love My son, Jesus…*John 17:23

*For in Jesus My love for you is revealed...*John 17:26

*He is the exact representation of My being...*Hebrews 1:3

*He came to demonstrate that I am for you, not against you...*Romans 8:31

And to tell you that I am not counting your sins...2 Corinthians 5:18-19

Jesus died so that you and I could be reconciled...2 Corinthians 5:18-19

His death was the ultimate expression of My love for you...1 John 4:10

*I gave everything that I loved that I might gain your love...*Romans 8:32

If you receive the gift of My Son, you receive Me...1 John 2:23

And nothing will ever separate you from My love again... Romans 8:38-39

*Come home and I will throw you the biggest party heaven has ever seen...*Luke 15:7

I have always been Father and will always be Father... Ephesians 3:14-15

*My question is...Will you be my child?...*John 1:12-13

*I am waiting for you...*Luke 15:11-32

> *Love, Your Dad*
> *Almighty God*[4]

Who does God say that I am? He says I am His child and He knows everything about me. He says that He chose me and desires to lavish His love on me. He says He rejoices over me with singing because I am treasured by Him. He says He has a plan for my life, and He is going to provide all that I need for that plan to be accomplished. He says that He will establish me and show me marvelous things. He says that He is my greatest encourager and my greatest source of comfort. He says that He has given me the most important gift of all, His love. That love was sent to me in the form of His Son, Jesus, Who came down from heaven to earth to die for my sin, so that I could be reconnected to the Father. He loves me that much! That is what God says about me. He says the same thing about you, my friend. And when you and I choose to identify with His Son Jesus, binding ourselves to Him, the treasures buried deep within us will begin to surface a little at a time. But first we must invite Him to rule over our hearts, select Him as the source of all our hope, and establish Him as the pathway to our eternal home.

Will you and I have it all together once we identify ourselves with Jesus? Hardly! But we will certainly be on our way. As I said before, it will take a lifetime to discover and uncover all that the Father has buried deep inside of us. But now that we possess a sure foundational understanding, we will be able to test all other definitions against that truth. When we believe what God says about us, we walk in the security of His purpose for our lives. And that security springs forth from a platform built on truth, not emotion, not speculation, and not assumption.

A DIVINE DEFINITION

Looking back into the plight of Sarah, we can see that she stepped into her agreement with Abraham for many reasons. She acted out of respect and honor for her beloved husband. She operated in fear and doubt about her uncertain future. She walked in ignorance and lack of understanding concerning the power of her God. When she fell into the trap set before her, she certainly had not grasped the magnitude of the importance of her life, or the assignment that had been placed on it. She was destined to be the mother of nations by birthing the child her God had promised. She chose to rely on her own definition of herself, along with the one provided by her husband. The lie concerning their relationship led Sarah and Abraham into separation and harm. But the lie was only the fruit of the root problem, a misunderstood identity. And until Sarah was set apart from the influence of others and shown how she appeared in the eyes and heart of Father God, she would not be able to change and become the woman she was destined to be. Sarah's hands were tied, and only the hand of God could untie such a knot. It was during these times of hiding that Sarah's reliance on the Father was strengthened and her resolve to believe in His promises was settled. Sarah saw herself as an old woman, unable to reproduce. Abraham saw her as his beloved wife and devoted sister. But the Father saw her as His child and the mother of nations, full of potential and pregnant with promise. It was in her darkest times that He chose to draw her close to Him, establishing His place in her heart and in her life. Then and only then was Sarah ready to face what lay ahead.

My friend, there is nothing missing. It is only hidden. And those things that have been hidden in you are there by the Father's design. When you and I allow Him to be the primary "Definer" of our lives, He equips and empowers us to face the future with hope and confidence. We will not have all the answers, but we will have the faithfulness and the guidance of the One who does. He will take us where we need to go. He will show us what we need to see.

So for now, when you sit in that warm, comfy room surrounded by several of your closest friends, and the conversation changes to those glorious questions about who you are and what you were created to do, what will you say? If you have chosen to identify with Jesus, you can say confidently that you are a treasured child of Father God. You can say boldly that He created you in love and designed you with a purpose. You can proclaim that His word about you is true, no matter what you may think, no matter what others might say. You can tell them that you are His and He is yours. He lives in and rules your heart. He is the source of all your hope. He is your way home.

Discussion Questions

1. Do you consider yourself one who has a balanced sense of self?

Explain.

2. Can you determine who is watching you, following you, and relying on you?

3. If there was one thing that you could leave as a legacy, what would it be? What changes would need to occur for this to happen?

4. It is easier for me to (build myself up/tear myself down).

Explain.

5. Name one negative label that others have used to describe you in the past. How has that label affected you? What can be done to erase it?

6. While reading the "Father's Love Letter," which description of you impacted you the most?

Why?

7. While reading the "Father's Love Letter," which description of you was the most difficult to believe?

Why?

8. Have you ever considered yourself pregnant with potential?

Explain.

CHAPTER FOUR

Weapon Two: Learn to Submit to Authority and to One Another

Remind people to be submissive to [their] *magistrates and authorities, to be obedient, to be prepared and willing to do any upright and honorable work, to slander or abuse or speak evil of no one, to avoid being contentious, to be forbearing (yielding, gentle, and conciliatory), and to show unqualified courtesy toward everybody.*

Titus 3:1-2

WHO NEEDS IT

Every weekday morning, it's the same thing. Jack, full of energy and raring to go, jumps into his car. Refusing to be tied down by the seat belt, he permits it to hang at his left side. The year-old makeshift sign explaining "tags applied for" still hangs where the license plate should, while the notice of insurance cancellation decorates the dash. He recklessly backs out of the driveway to begin his daily adventure to work. Once again, he ignores the stop sign at the corner, drives fifteen miles above the posted limit, and rides the tail of any driver who, by some unfortunate chain of events, happens to get in his way. As he nears the parking lot, he checks to make sure that his favorite place is not occupied. Noting its availability, he swerves into the favored spot marked "disabled permit parking only." Jack dismounts, making sure the car doors are locked, deterring anyone who is not a law-abiding citizen like himself from entering and destroying his personal property. Then he heads to his office, confident that all the decisions he makes today will be "right."

You and I might have a good laugh at this exaggerated story, but the message behind it rings true for many of us.

41

We just don't want to believe it or admit it. Under the surface lies the possibility that you and I may possess a tendency to think that the need for authority, rules, and regulations is geared toward those who don't know any better. We, on the other hand, instinctively know right from wrong and live our lives accordingly. We are responsible people needing little, if any, limitations or governing from outside sources. There is no need to lecture us on the need for order and the importance of boundaries, for we are civilized, intelligent people. You and I may have come to the conclusion that submission is not an issue for us but for those who suffer from lack of self-control. If so, we have been fooling ourselves. We have misunderstood the purpose of authority and the need for all, not just a select few, to submit to it.

MISUNDERSTOOD

A surefire way to begin an argument with some people, maybe most people, is to strike up a conversation concerning the subject of submission. Submission could easily make the top ten list of "Issues Most Misunderstood by Man." It has been the match that fired many a conversation, resulting in unnecessary strife and pointless division. How could something so fitting, so sensible, and so necessary be so misunderstood? To submit is to choose to give honor and respect where it is due. It says, "I am willing to listen, to try to understand, to negotiate. At times, I am willing to back down and trust your judgment when we do not see eye to eye. At other times, I am willing to wait until we do." That is submission.

Though this concept appears very natural, and even simple, it has become suspect to many. It is as if submitting to one another would be equal to intentionally walking into a jail cell, locking the door behind us, and handing over the key, never to see daylight again. We believe that when we finally weaken and let someone else have even a small degree of "control" over any area of our lives, an evil-looking cloud settles overhead with one purpose: to dominate and oppress. In today's society, submission is viewed as a sign of weakness that warrants strong resistance. It is charged with imprisoning its participants and stifling freedom of expression. How did we get such a distorted view of submission? Why have we considered it to be an act of not only giving in, but also one of completely giving up?

There is no question that in many instances submission is giving in. It is giving in to another's plans, passions, and desires above our own. It is giving in for the purpose of advancing the whole, instead of holding on with self-advancement in mind. It is giving permission to make the final decision, or adhering to an existing rule. Genuine submission requires giving in and handing over our wants, ideas, and opinions, but it never demands giving up. To give up means to be without hope in the situation. That is not the purpose of submission. Submission is expressing honor and respect while believing in and relying on hope, resulting in love and unity. We must not submit without hope, but rest in hope in order to submit. And who is our hope? Jesus is our hope.

MISREPRESENTED

Submission does not operate alone; it partners with authority. Authority is the glove that fits over the hand called submission. Sometimes the glove fits suitably, and sometimes it does not. Whatever the case, authority has been given by God for the purpose of protection, never invasion or attack. To be given authority is to be granted "the right to give orders, make decisions, or take action." [5] It is a privilege. Over the centuries, *authority* has been misused. Countless victims have fallen under the tyranny of another whose pride and lust for power has overcome all compassion. And it is compassion that invites complete and voluntary submission. Nothing draws people to authority faster than a genuine desire to provide help in their time of need.

Jesus is the ultimate authority. While He walked on this earth, multitudes were drawn to Him. Many came to be fed. Others came to be healed. Some came just to satisfy their curiosity. But all came out of need. When Jesus saw the people, He was moved with compassion. Now, tell me, is He someone to whom you and I could readily submit? If you and I have had any experience under His care at all, we know that He does not use His authority to force us into anything, but allows us to make our own choices. In other words, we hold the "choice" key. To step under the authority of Jesus is freeing, strengthening, and encircling. Why? It is His desire to help us by guiding us, by knowing what is best for us, and by taking action on our behalf. Yes, Jesus is the ultimate authority, but the heavenly Father has also elected to empower additional overseers for our protection.

The Father has established every authority figure in every home, every city, every state, every country, and every church. These authorities are ordinary people of all ages, all cultures, and all denominations. There is not one who has not been divinely appointed by Him. And yet many of them do not fit the hand of submission favorably; their attitude and actions make it difficult for us to obey. Why? There are several reasons. First, there are those who insist on controlling others, void of compassion. They have taken their God-given appointment and turned it into a license to overpower and oppress. Their concept of submission is distorted and will only be tolerated by the Father for a time, and then restitution will come. Then there are those who have yet to understand what compassion looks like. They undoubtedly desire to do what is right with the responsibility they have been given, but lack the understanding concerning the power of, and the need for, compassion. Instead, they do their best by attempting every technique and formula available, hoping for favorable results. For them, the idea of compassion almost seems too simple; but once all else is exhausted they will return to it, desire to understand it, and eventually learn to walk in it. In addition, there are those who are learning how to walk in and express compassion freely. For many, the desire to help someone in need does not come naturally. It is a learned behavior requiring not only the refocusing of time and talents, but also requiring the transparency and humility necessary to express human emotion freely. Both requirements come at a price.

You see, my friend, it is all about compassion. Without compassion, walking in a position of authority becomes a challenge, both for the authority and for those who have been placed under their care. Challenge or no challenge, we are commanded by the Father to submit to authority and to one another. To choose otherwise is to rebel, not only against authority, but also against God Himself!

GIVING HONOR, SHOWING RESPECT

Having discussed what authority is and why we must learn to submit to it, let us talk briefly about who our authorities are and how we can put submission into action. Remember that an authority is someone who has been selected to care for us. An authority can hold an office in the government, like the President, the governor, or the mayor. An authority can hold a position of service, like the police or firefighters. Authorities can also stand in positions not related to the government: in schools as principals and teachers, in churches as pastors and elders, at job sites as owners and supervisors, and in homes as parents and husbands. Each position requires that we show respect and honor with our actions and in our words. How do we do that? What are some practical ways we can show our respect? How do we take action?

The first action step you and I can take, whether we have relationship with the authority or not, is to openly recognize their God-given position. When we choose to look at those who have been given the responsibility of our care as being appointed by God, we will be able to focus more on the position, and less on the person in that position. Why would we want to do that? One reason is that people make mistakes; God does not. When we put our total trust in the person and not the position, then hurt and disappointment are inevitable, whether intended or not. Does this mean all people in authority will be a disappointment? No. It means that there is the possibility of disappointment along the way. Therefore, if we put our total trust in God, the Creator and Sustainer of the position and the person, we can expect healing and growth to result during those times of hurt and disappointment. Believe it or not, these times of healing and growth will prove to usher us into a whole new level of respect and honor: first for the position, and then for the person.

Another reason for focusing on the position instead of the person is that we are human, and we have a tendency to lean on others in an unhealthy way without even realizing it. When a wise and caring authority fills a place of need in our lives, their opinions have the potential of becoming more important to us than they should. If this takes place, we run the risk of relying on the authority more and God less. This is a precarious position, to say the least. It will not be long before the Lord steps in to reclaim His rightful place, either by revelation or by separation. When we recognize our authorities as elected and positioned by God and respect the position first and the person next, we give honor where honor is due.

The second step we can take in putting submission into action is to obey the laws that have been established by our authorities. This seems to be a challenge for our friend Jack. He does not yet understand the importance of adhering to the laws that have been established by the authorities of the land. He does not comprehend the fact that the laws were set in place for the purpose of his safety, as well as the safety of those around him. He, in fact, has chosen to rebel against the established laws and is willing to take the risk of hurting someone else, ignoring the cost. Rebellion has many faces: Sometimes it is blatantly obvious as with our friend Jack, sometimes it is tolerably subtle, and sometimes it is innocently unrecognized. Whatever its form, it is rebellion just the same.

How about you and me? Where do we stand on adhering to the law of the land, the guidelines at work, or the boundaries at home? Obeying the established law, guidelines, and boundaries puts submission into action. It says that we have chosen to honor and respect. Rebelling against them, in whatever shape or form, says that we have chosen to dishonor and disrespect the decisions put into place by the people God has elected. What if we do not agree with what has been established by authority? What do we do then? Whenever possible, we voice our opinion, suggesting another option. There is no rebellion in wanting to be heard. There is no rebellion in making suggestions. But once we have had our say, we are to relinquish the final decision to those who are held responsible.

The third, and possibly the most powerful, action step we can take is to speak highly of our authorities. There is power in the tongue. It has the power to bless or the power to curse. It can encourage and bring life to a situation, or it can discourage and bring death. It can build up, or it can tear down. Let me ask you, would you rather be known as one who builds or as one who demolishes? Some of us have the mistaken idea that to speak well of someone automatically communicates that we agree with everything that person does or says. That is far from the truth. To speak well of someone is to speak well of someone. To agree with someone is to agree with someone. Neither relies nor depends on the other. You and I must focus on what is good about those who have accepted the awesome responsibility of caring for us, by speaking out words that will build them up, not only in their eyes, but also in the eyes of others. When we choose to encourage others from a submissive heart, then we will be able to consider ourselves to be "people builders."

Giving Care, Showing Love

We are commanded not only to submit to those who hold positions of authority, but also to submit to one another (see Ephesians 5:21). While for some it is difficult to learn how to submit to authority, for others it is even more of a challenge learning to operate in submission toward another. The idea of giving in to someone who holds no office of power or position seems to go against the grain. Here are a few suggestions to help the learning process along for those who find this area of submission challenging.

First, seek to see people as God sees them. People will always be people. They come in all shapes and sizes, all types of personalities, and all levels of maturity. Inside every one lies a past, a passion, and a pursuit. Each carries hopes and dreams, heartache and disappointment. Each is unique and complex in nature, yet similar and simple in need. Each hungers to be loved, yearns to belong, and aspires to contribute. We all fundamentally desire the same goals, yet many of us get deterred, if not lost, along the way. With that in mind, you and I can help to make a difference. We can seek to see each person not as they appear but as God sees them. How does He see them? Remember the "Father's Love Letter" we read in chapter three? That is how He sees them. Take a moment and refer back to what God says about those He has created and ask Him to allow you to see them as He does. Then wait, expecting to receive insight and revelation from Him.

Second, allow others to have an opinion. Everyone has something to say and everyone wants to be heard. Listening (not just hearing, but listening with the intent to understand) to another invites openness and transparency, promoting friendship and establishing a platform of mutual respect. What could be better than that? Listening to someone says, "You are important and what you have to say is important." The next time you find yourself in a position where you and another must come to an agreement, try listening intently. Set your feelings and ideas aside for the moment and open your heart. Who knows, you may learn something and bless someone in the process!

Once you have listened to someone and understood their wishes, what would it take for you to honor those wishes? This is the third suggestion under the topic of submitting to one another: to honor the wishes of others. When we are very young, we learn that it is gratifying to get our own way, not just some of the time, but all of the time. As we grow and mature, we discover that getting our way is not always possible. So, what do we do? We learn to choose our battles. What do I mean by that? There comes a time in life when we must draw a line of demarcation. It is the line that says these are the areas open to negotiation, but these are not. Then each time a circumstance presents itself, we are able to hold it up against that line and determine if it is worth fighting for. Soon we discover that when we honor the wishes of others, it is seldom a threat to anything but our pride. Understanding our own wishes and their importance to us, along with understanding our human bent toward wanting our way, is the beginning of learning the art of honoring the wishes of others.

Submission, Testimony of Choice

Our main character of study, Sarah, understood the act of submission extremely well. In her day, rebellion against the authority of the land could easily have resulted in the death penalty. Authority was not something to tamper with, whether fueled by compassion or not. Sarah understood that very well. And when she found herself under the rule and power of a foreign king, she knew how to handle herself submissively and reverently. I wonder how well you and I would have handled this most undesirable situation. Would we have given in as easily as Sarah did, or would we have gone kicking and screaming, demanding our rights, refusing to comply? I wonder.

I also wonder if we would have responded to Abraham's request as favorably as Sarah did. Agreeing to be less than who we are is no pleasant task. And yet Sarah did just that. Why did she? There was always the possibility of an alternate plan: Turn and run, tell the truth and risk death, or hope that God would override the famine by sending manna down daily as He had faithfully done in the past. Why did she do it? She did it because her husband asked her to do it. She chose to honor him by allowing him to make the final decision. We do not know how she felt about it. We only know how she acted upon it: with submission. And that selfless act of submission has become a testimony to all who read of her today.

When we learn to submit to people in positions of authority and when we learn to submit to one another, a wonderful thing happens. It may not come instantly. It may not come in the way we expect it. But it will surely come. What is it? It is the blessing of God. Why? God's blessing comes when we choose to obey His commands. May you and I seek to become less and less like our friend Jack, and more and more like Abraham's Sarah, trusting in the Lord who sets all authority into place and believing in His ability to protect us and provide all of our needs.

The Radical View

We began this chapter with the distorted view of submission. You may recall the jail cell, the locked door, the surrendered key, and the sentence of darkness. Call me radical, but the cell door I once dreaded I now clearly see as a gate inviting us to go in. The key we hold is the key called "choice" used to open and close the gate at any time. The jail cell we have envisioned is actually a field overflowing with provision: grass to eat, water to drink, and space to run freely, yet safely. The dark cloud hovering over us is the enemy in his feeble attempt to discourage us with his threats of darkness. And in spite of the impressive display, his power cannot match the might of the One who oversees the field and all that it contains. Submission is not weakening, but strengthening. It is not stifling, but freeing. It is not imprisoning, but encircling.

DISCUSSION QUESTIONS

1. In regard to submission, I identify more with…
   a. Our friend Jack
   b. Those who believe it is not an issue for them.

Explain.

2. I have viewed submission to authority in the past as…
   a. Dominating and suppressing.
   b. Imprisoning; justifying resistance.
   c. Giving up; rendering hopelessness.
   d. Honoring and respecting.
   e. Protecting and providing.

Explain.

3. One authority figure in my life that could be considered as the glove not fitting well is…

Explain.

4. One authority figure in my life that could be considered as the glove fitting well is…

Explain.

5. What are some examples of subtle rebellion?

6. Is there an authority figure in your life of whom you have spoken negatively in the past? What can you do about it now? How can you avoid it in the future?

7. I tend to be most challenged with…
    a. Seeing people as God sees them.
    b. Listening with the intent to understand.
    c. Developing a line of demarcation for negotiation.

8. My first step in becoming a more submissive person will be to….

CHAPTER FIVE

Weapon Three: Learn To Serve All People

...whoever wishes to be great among you must be your servant, and whoever desires to be first among you must be your slave—Just as the Son of Man came not to be waited on but to serve, and to give His life as a ransom for many [the price paid to set them free].

Matthew 20:26-28

What's in a Name?

If I were to ask you to name someone you know and admire who personifies your definition of a servant, who would that person be? Take a moment and seriously think about it, allowing a name to come to mind. Now, permit me to ask you a few questions concerning your choice.

First, what is it about this person that prompts you to view them as one who serves? Is it their willingness to always be available anytime, day or night? Is it their eagerness to lend a hand no matter what the task, big or small? Is it the way they are able to make others feel important, understood, and cared for? What makes this person's approach different?

Second, what actions has this person taken in the past that placed them in such a position of honor in your eyes? Did your view of them result from one single life-changing event, a steady consistent stream of selfless acts, or a few small incidents? What warrants your viewing them as an example of servanthood?

Third, if you could attain one character trait from this person of service, what would that trait be? Do you want to be able to handle situations more patiently? Do you want to learn how to deal with others more compassionately? Do you desire the ability to give more freely and more readily? What trait would you desire?

When you and I honestly answer these questions, taking note of what is uncovered, we will ultimately conclude that servants are people who have learned how to influence others in a positive way. How? They do it by adjusting their schedules, allowing flexibility and spontaneity. They do it by surrendering all that they are and all that they will be into the hands of God. They are people who have allowed Him to cultivate patience, compassion, and selflessness in their lives. Godly servants know that serving others is all about handling them patiently, dealing with them compassionately, and giving to them freely and readily.

It is unfortunate that some do not necessarily serve with the right heart motives. These people may have misled you and me in the past. They busied themselves with many tasks, filling every need as it surfaced. They sacrificed their time and talents for the sake of doing for others, never tiring or complaining. They kept themselves informed at all times for the sake of being involved. And although these activities are viewed as helpful and good, they sometimes are motivated by an incentive other than compassion. The incentive I am speaking of is self-importance.

At times in the past, and sometimes in the present if I am not careful, I have found myself serving out of self-importance instead of out of compassion. With the very best of intentions, I have busied myself completing task after task, tallying my successes one by one, with little thought of helping others. The truth was that each successfully completed task represented another notch in my belt, another good deed to be counted when the time came to compare scores. I stayed one step ahead, not only because it was natural for my personality but also because it made me look good in the eyes of others. I served out of a desire to please God, but I also "served" out of a desire to look good and please myself. I was performing the part of a servant, not being a servant. Instead of filling the needs of others and investing in their lives, I found myself investing in my own selfish needs. I had been misled. If it is possible for you and me to deceive ourselves so easily, how can we tell if we are performing the "servant," or being a servant? In other words, what makes a servant a servant?

Profile of a Servant
A Servant Recognizes the Needs of Others.

We do not have to look very far to see people in need. Physical, mental, emotional, and spiritual lack plagues many in our world today. Take Jane's family for example. Jane, a single mom, works two jobs, leaving little time for her five children. Her eldest son, Matt, is beginning to show signs of depression. He sees himself responsible for the financial needs of the family, being the man and all, but he has not been able to find a part-time job that pays enough to supplement his mother's income. The baby, Michael, cries out for his mother's attention by biting the other kids in preschool. He just wants to be at home with his mommy. The two older girls, Marcy and Mary, show promising signs of creativity and talent, but have no way to express them and no one to help develop them. And then there is the youngest girl, Maggie. Maggie lives in a world of her own. She just wants to be invisible, hoping not to be a bother to anyone. Jane finds herself in a place she never expected to be, in need. Every night as she lies down to go to sleep, she wonders how she is going to make it through another day.

In another house lies Jake, wiping away the tears that continue to dampen his face. It was exactly one week ago that the phone rang with the heartrending news. Jenny, his wife of two years, had gone out to get some coffee with a friend who was in need of some consoling. On her way back home a truck ran a red light and hit her car on the driver's side. The car was totaled. The police report said that Jenny had died instantly upon impact. She did not suffer. Jake cannot say the same for himself. He suffers in a way that he cannot possibly explain, and his mind never rests. Imagining the accident over and over in his head, he entertains all the what-ifs until he falls asleep in exhaustion. He awakens only to encounter the overwhelming emptiness and unbearable grief once again. How is he ever going to get through this? How will he ever be able to live without his Jenny?

Ted and Tammy find themselves wondering about the future much like Jane and Jake. They do not struggle with the responsibilities of raising children. Ted and Tammy have no children. Both are successful career people climbing the corporate ladder, fulfilling childhood dreams and aspirations. They have their work and they have each other. Or do they? As of late, Ted has become distant and less attentive than usual and Tammy is beginning to see herself as less attractive to her husband. Something has created a rift between the two of them, though neither one dares to broach the subject. Ted keeps to himself most of the time while Tammy waits, imagining the worst.

We all need reminding from time to time that there are those who are in need and that you and I may have what it takes to fill that need. It could be as simple as giving someone a job. It could be as complicated as taking someone into our home and caring for them for the rest of his life. Can we provide help for everyone? No, it would be ridiculous to even try. Sometimes helping can mean jumping in with both feet. Sometimes helping can mean staying out of the way. In order to make a difference, you and I need to learn how to recognize the particular needs in any given situation and decide how we might be able to help. How do we do that? First, we adjust our focus from being self-minded to being other-minded. Second, we develop a willingness to see not only those things that lie on the surface but also those things that have settled underneath. Third, we ask God what we can do to help.

A SERVANT READILY HELPS OTHERS.

It is one thing to be willing to see the needs of others, but it is quite another thing to be willing to act upon what we see. In many cases, to help another will mean letting go of any fear we might be holding onto. "What fears?" you ask.

There is the fear of getting in over our head, making things worse instead of better. There is the fear of failing to achieve what we set out to do and as a result losing the good opinion and respect of those who might be watching. There is the fear of succeeding in what we set out to do, not knowing if we can handle the success without pride settling in. There is the fear of what others might say about us. And there is the fear of what others might not say about us. There is the fear of losing affirmation and confirmation from those who would normally support us. There is the fear of being taken advantage of. There is the fear of getting trapped in the middle of something unfavorable. There is the fear of getting involved and getting too close. And there is the fear of getting too close and then having to let go.

Acting upon the needs that we see will mean letting go and letting Someone larger than ourselves take over. When we say no to our fears, we open the door of opportunity, the opportunity to serve. A servant does not think about failing or succeeding, but about serving. He is not concerned with what others might say or think or do, but with what pleases his Father in heaven. He is not driven by affirmation or confirmation, but propelled by inspiration and revelation. He invites the chance to get close to others, knowing that in the process he also will emerge as one who is blessed. Selflessness, compassion, and obedience are the primary motivators for a servant. His only desire is to impact God's Kingdom so that it might grow, advance, and ultimately glorify Him.

A SERVANT DELIGHTS IN INVESTING IN THE LIVES OF OTHERS.

To serve others in their time of need, whatever that need may be, is to make an investment. An investment deposited into a life is in turn an investment deposited into the lives of each and every person who is touched by that life. A servant knows that it is a privilege to work for the dreams and passions of others. He understands that at times he will be asked to set aside his own desires for the sake of another, expecting no reward from it other than the pleasure of knowing that the life of another has been encouraged and enhanced. A servant is willing to wait for his reward in Heaven. By first serving here, he stores up his treasures there. How do I know if I am a servant or not? I am a true servant if I am not offended when people treat me like one.

Serving is all about others. It is the result of compassion for others. First the heart sees the need and desires to make a difference, then the hands attempt to meet the need in love and with mercy. Serving others is never to be used as a vehicle for personal gain but rather as a means of expressing love from one to another. It is never to be viewed as conditional but as unrestricted, unattached, and free from all conditions. It is never to be taken for granted but to be realized and treasured as a gift from the heart. Wherever there is a servant reaching out and distributing love, in one form or another, there is a recipient of that love.

You and I are recipients of the most compassionate love known to man. The love I speak of originated in the heart of, and expressed itself through the selfless actions of, the greatest servant of all, Jesus. He tells us in His Word that serving was His purpose for being on earth; He came to serve and not to be served. His was the perfect example of a ministry propelled by compassion and delivered to those who needed it the most: the lost, the sick, the hungry, the deaf, the blind, and the hurting. It delighted Him to be the dispenser of love and mercy to those who lacked, whether they appreciated it or not. And by the power of His love, the lost were led, the sick were healed, the hungry were fed, the deaf received hearing, the blind received sight, and the hurting were consoled. If there is any name that rightly deserves the title of servant, it is the name of Jesus. He was, and is, the greatest servant of all.

SERVANTHOOD FROM HEAD TO TOE

There is no greater love than to lay down your life for another (see John 15:13). Sarah did not hear these words as

Jesus preached them and she did not read them in the Word written long after her time on this earth; but, nevertheless, she lived them. Void of the drive for personal gain and free from all conditions, Sarah saw the need at hand and expressed her love for her husband by putting not only her hands to the task, but also her entire being. She saw the need and her heart summoned her to fill it. Was she oblivious to the possible danger facing her? No. Was she sure that laying aside her dreams and desires guaranteed her success in trying to save their lives? No. Did she have any idea that her decision to serve her husband in this particular way would bring about what God had promised? No, but she chose to do it anyway.

The Army of God could use a few more soldiers like Sarah! It needs people who are willing to let go of personal agendas and support someone else. It needs people who are willing to invest in the dreams of another at the risk of delaying or even erasing their own. This is not an easy task, especially when compassion-filled hearts lay idle, impatiently waiting to explode into action; heads race unceasingly with ideas and dreams, anxiously looking for an opportunity to move ahead; and hands that long to reach out, hang down at sides, aching to touch. To set aside a natural inclination and yearning for the sake of another might seem unfair, even a form of torment to some. Yet while you and I work faithfully and selflessly tending the vineyard of another (investing), the Lord is at work tending ours.

Looking Back

Let us take a look back to where we have come from up to this point. We discovered the current state of the Army of God and the need for those who have been hidden to prepare to step up and step out at the instruction of the Commander in Chief, King Jesus. We established in chapter one what it means to be hidden, and walked through the pages of time investigating the lives of others who dealt with times of hiddenness and the presence and purpose of the

Lord during those times. Each example of a hidden season in the life of these people proved to be a time set aside to be intimate with the Lord. We examined the life of Abraham and Sarah and how they chose to handle the results of a difficult decision, in chapter two. We discovered that in the midst of it all Sarah was forced to reach out beyond her own abilities and receive weapons of spiritual warfare. The weapons we uncovered were the various weapons of humility. In chapter three, we began to look at the weapons, one by one, beginning with a challenge to believe in our God-given identity. We then, in chapter four, expanded our understanding of submission, explaining the power behind it and the command to walk in it. And finally, in this chapter, we took a peek at the ministry of serving others. These are just a few of the weapons of humility brought out of the arsenal in the account of Abraham and Sarah. Now let us reach in and take out the fourth weapon of humility: waiting on the Lord to reveal your identity.

DISCUSSION QUESTIONS

1. Which best describes you?

   a. I cannot see the needs of others at this time because of my own overwhelming needs.

   b. I see the needs of others but do not know how I can help them.

   c. I see the needs of others and want to help them all, but can't.

Explain.

2. I admit I have a fear of....

3. Others could help me overcome my fears by....

4. Make a list of those things about you that might be worth investing into the lives of others.

5. What steps can you take to begin to invest in one life today?

6. Can you think of another account in the Bible where someone laid down his life for another?

7. What best describes your current state?

   a. The compassion-filled heart lying idle waiting to explode into action

   b. The head full of ideas and dreams looking for an opportunity to move ahead

   c. The hands longing to reach out and aching to touch another

d. The soldier on the front lines needing support from others

e. The servant investing in the dream of another at the risk of your own

8. What do you see as the difference between "performing the servant" and being the servant?

CHAPTER SIX

Weapon Four: Wait on the Lord to Reveal Your Identity

Wait and hope for and expect the Lord; be brave and of good courage and let your heart be stout and enduring. Yes, wait for and hope for and expect the Lord.

Psalm 27:14

WHAT NOT TO DO

Do you remember the story *The Emperor's New Clothes*? If not, let me refresh your memory. The story begins with an emperor who, out of nothing more than greed, commissioned a team of traveling tailors to design a new wardrobe for him. Rumor had it that the material they carried was not only beautiful to the eye but also possessed a unique quality in that it could only be seen by the wise. The newly employed tailors apparently stayed busy day and night fulfilling the desires of their employer. After great anticipation, the time arrived for the results of the hard work to be conveyed from the hands of the tailors to the back of the emperor for final fitting and adjustments. Piece by piece the emperor tried on his new clothing, responding to the tailors' unceasing adoration with delight, all the while fighting the negative thoughts that tormented his mind. To his disappointment and dismay, he was unable to see the remarkable "discerning" cloth. Admitting his failure would mean disclosing his lack of wisdom, and that was unacceptable. So he chose to play along. Prancing around in front of his full-length mirror, he was found admiring the "missing" clothing whenever he could release his eyes from admiring himself. Filled with pride and driven by fear, he declared the venture a success. As a result, he decided that the new and improved wardrobe must be put on display for the entire kingdom to view and appreciate. Plans were made and the people were publicly notified of the upcoming fashion show featuring the emperor himself. Eagerness grew as the people waited for the castle doors to open and their well-dressed leader to appear. The moment finally arrived and the emperor made his long-awaited entrance. To his delight the people expressed their amazement, falling into complete and utter silence. Slowly at first, then progressively faster, they began to applaud the artistry of the tailors as it made its way down Main Street hanging on the royal frame. The people cheered with excitement. The tailors sighed with relief. The emperor sashayed with shameless pride.

The story could have ended there, allowing everyone the temporary pleasure that performance often brings, but it did not. Instead, it continued with a boy found standing stunned and confused. Refusing to accept what he was witnessing in this colorful yet unbelievable parade and unwilling to participate in such a farce, he yelled out above the crowd, "He hasn't any clothes on!" And he was right. The royal parade promising its audience the latest in fine clothing essentially consisted of nothing more than undergarments serving as minimal cover over the emperor's maximum form. The story leaves us with the tailors' scheming ways uncovered, the emperor's lack of wisdom displayed, the people's weakness of character exposed, and the boy's impetuous candor exhibited.

We should thank Mr. Andersen for making it effortless to relate to the characters that he has created in this story. First there are the tailors. These are men who promote themselves as something they are not. They specialize in getting something for nothing, unwilling to pay the price. Then there is the emperor who is full of nothing but self. A little bit of flattery thrown his way gets quickly soaked up, allowing room for more. When it comes to admiration and approval, he is insatiable and incapable of admitting any faults or weaknesses. Then there are the crowds of people who see the truth, know better than to promote the lie, but choose to do so regardless of the consequences. They fear being different and choose to conform to what is expected, and in doing so they settle for less. And finally, there is the boy. He sees the truth and speaks it out, exhibiting the fearlessness and zeal of youth. Unfortunately, instead of making the situation better, he made it worse. In his zeal to correct the matter, he acted out of emotion rather than wisdom, leaving the emperor standing in the midst of his subjects exposed and humiliated. Self-promotion, self-preoccupation, self-preservation, and self-appointment all help to make this story an excellent example of what not to do in the midst of life's difficult situations.

TRAPPED BY SELF-PROMOTION

In our world today we are told that in order to get ahead we must do all we can to promote ourselves. For the sake of advancement we embellish resumes, inflate abilities and talents, and conveniently drop a few impressive names, all the while considering such practices to be necessary and acceptable. The dilemma with this mentality is deciding where to draw the line. How much do we embellish? How much do we inflate? How many names do we drop? Who sets the standard?

Our friends the tailors are an exaggerated yet prime example of self-promotion carried to the extreme. These are people who set out to obtain a job by promoting themselves as tailors; yet in the end, there was much evidence to the contrary. The evidence we see is that they have been deceived. They have allowed themselves to believe that if they did not "sell" themselves, no one else would. Their mentality was that of the survival of the fittest: "I must get mine before someone else does." They permitted themselves to fall into the trap of expecting payment and reward without having to go through the process of working for it or waiting for it. By doing so, they deprived themselves of the opportunity to grow. Without the process of growth, any reward that is obtained will soon be mishandled and eventually fade away.

It is evident that our tailor friends were not able to wait for anything or anyone to help them along on their path. Hopefully, their "revealing" experience with the emperor was a lesson learned: Self-promotion does not pay.

TRAPPED BY SELF-PREOCCUPATION

Many of the books that line the shelves of bookstores and most of the commercials we see on television today deal with the topic of indulging ourselves. We are told that certain products are necessary in order for our lives to amount to anything and that to ignore such products would be detrimental. We have been trained to believe in the importance of showing our best and hiding our worst. While a degree of caution in life is appropriate, an excess of caution for the sake of dignity and pride could prove to be an even greater weakness than the ones we are attempting to hide. Take the emperor for example.

While the tailors were busy promoting themselves, the emperor was completely occupied with admiring himself. He was so full of pride that he not only loved looking at himself, he wanted to share his beauty, his good fortune, and his immeasurable intelligence with others less fortunate. He would do anything for attention, including a one-man fashion show. But just as the show reached its finale, a piercing voice broke out from the midst of his devoted fans. The underlying message went something like this, "Open your eyes and take a good look at yourself!" At that moment pride took off running and humiliation jumped in. For the sake of the emperor, we can only hope that he was able to recover from his uncomfortable time of "brief exposure." Undoubtedly, the time he spent in front of the mirror from then on held a whole new meaning for him. He learned the hard way that self-admiration and excessive self-indulgence eventually lead to humiliation.

TRAPPED BY SELF-PRESERVATION

There is a condition that plagues the lives of many today. It crawls in slowly, taking over little areas of interest at first, then steadily seeps into the most important issues of all: issues connected to faith, to hope, and to love. The name of this immobilizing condition is complacency. Once invited in, complacency has the power to disarm passion and courage while heavily arming apathy and compromise. Its goal is to imprison and paralyze anyone who might be willing to step forward and make a difference. The emperor's subjects showed obvious symptoms of this subtle and damaging condition.

While the tailors sat rooted in self-promotion and the emperor stood blinded in self-preoccupation, the crowds walked willingly into self-preservation. Unlike the tailors and the Emperor, the crowds were not deceived. They knew exactly what they were doing: saving their hides! Confronted with the choice of speaking out or being quiet, they chose to be quiet. Confronted with the challenge of being different from the rest or conforming, they chose to conform. And in doing so, they walked into the trap of self-preservation; ignoring the truth and placing value in the lie. Self-preservation hooks its prey by threatening harm and ridicule. It knows that the tendency of every man, woman, and child is to avoid anything that might possibly inflict pain or result in rejection. It persuades people to shrink back when they should press forward, to keep quiet when they should speak out, and to conform when they should be different. The trap called self-preservation continues to snare its victims over and over again until they discover themselves alone and hurting in the one place they were desperately trying to avoid. We do not know what happened to the crowds once the truth was revealed. Did they admit that they might have been more forthcoming about what they did or didn't see? Did they show respect and compassion by providing a coat or a blanket to cover their distressed leader? Did they excuse themselves in yet another attempt to preserve their self-made reputations? Did they come to the conclusion that self-preservation is a sure path to immobilization?

TRAPPED BY SELF-APPOINTMENT

If only the energy and the eagerness of the young could be bottled and sold! It would definitely be a best-seller. Not that energy and enthusiasm are complete in themselves. They require the balancing that maturity and experience contribute. Where youth and inexperience may step out propelled by emotion, maturity will wait for the right timing. Where maturity may hesitate in fear because of past unpleasant experiences, youth proceeds with fearlessness. The youngest character in our story exhibited not only great courage but also great promise.

In contrast to the crowds, the boy in our story had no reservations about expressing himself. In many cases, his response would have been the most appropriate action to take. Regrettably, this was not one of those cases. This young man recognized the truth easily enough and in his heart he knew something needed to be done. Replying to his heart's cry and releasing his emotions, he made a decision that would prove damaging to everyone involved. In this delicate and potentially volatile situation he decided to appoint himself "town crier," proclaiming what he saw to be true. Unknowingly, this precious boy walked right into a trap. The name of the trap that seized him that day was the trap of self-appointment. This trap proved to be the most destructive because it ruthlessly attracted the innocent and caused confusion among the masses. In the end, the boy's words not only uncovered the scheme of the tailors; they also uncovered the nakedness of the emperor and the complacency of the crowd. He was about to learn a lesson that would prove to be priceless in the future: that when one is given the ability to see something and to understand it, he is not necessarily the one to reveal it to others.

The characters we encountered in this story were different in many ways yet shared one thing. Each one struggled with an issue of self: self-promotion, self-preoccupation, self-preservation, or self-appointment. And although the assorted struggles were expressed in a variety of ways, they stemmed from the same root cause. The tailors, the emperor, the crowds of people, and the boy all acted out of human need: the need to be seen, the need to be heard, the need to be accepted, and the need to be understood. Who can blame them for that? I want the same things, don't you? We all do. We just don't know how to go about obtaining them. So we try campaigning ourselves into high-profile positions by proclaiming to be something we are not. We try indulging our wants and desires and then parading around for others to see. We try protecting our reputations at the risk of undermining our integrity. We try to insure that what we have to say is heard by anyone who will listen. And we do it all because we want to be seen. We want to be heard. We want to be accepted. And we want to be understood. You and I are no different from the characters we met in this fable. In many cases, we have believed that we must play along with the world in order for our needs to be met.

Sarah Revealed

Sarah dealt with the same frustration. Needing desperately to be seen, she found herself in a place where she was practically invisible. Needing more than anything to be heard, she lost any voice in regard to her present or her future. Needing to be unconditionally accepted, she suffered rejection from her own people. Needing to be understood, she found herself not only misunderstood but also treated unjustly. One day she was the matriarch of the nation she so dearly loved, and the next day she was of no reputation at all. Sarah had only one thing to do: wait. Wait for a breakthrough. Wait for a sign. Wait for a miracle. And when it seemed as if all hope was gone, her wait came to an end. Seeing her when she was all but invisible, hearing her inner cry for help, accepting her in spite of all her weaknesses, and understanding her better than she understood herself, Father God came to her rescue. No, He did not unlock the gate so she could sneak out on her own. No, He did not make a way for Abraham to climb the wall and retrieve her. No, He did not bring about an earthquake to swallow up those who had taken her captive. He came to the king who held her prisoner and spoke to him in a dream (see Genesis 20:3). In that dream God revealed who Sarah was. The king was warned firmly yet lovingly that it would go well for him and his kingdom if he chose to treat her with honor and respect by releasing her to her husband.

Sarah waited. Yes, we could make the statement that she had no other choice in the matter, and we would be right. But Sarah was given much more than her freedom that day. She was given a weapon: the weapon of waiting on the Lord. Because of that weapon Sarah would be able to approach difficult times in the future with a confidence that was planted, rooted, and established (see Colossians 2:7). God had delivered her out of what seemed to be a hopeless state, and in that delivery she discovered that with Him all things are possible for those who wait (see Matthew 19:26).

SOLDIERS IN WAITING

Waiting is one of the most difficult challenges you and I must face. We are called to wait on promotion and advancement in every area of our lives (see James 5:7; Isaiah 64:4). We are called to wait on what brings satisfaction by focusing on growing in wisdom instead (see Psalm 90:12; Proverbs 2:6-7; Proverbs 8:11). We are called to wait on and believe in God's protection as we stand up for truth (see Psalm 25:5, 21). We are called to wait for appointment and the fulfillment it promises to bring (see Psalm 37:9, 34). We are called to wait on all of these things because that is what a soldier does (see 2 Timothy 2:3-4).

No officer would allow the promotion or advancement of a soldier until he had been trained, no matter what the soldier thought or felt. No officer would focus more on the satisfaction of his troops than on their training and preparation for war. No officer would permit his soldiers to go into battle without providing every available protection. No officer would appoint responsibilities to a soldier who had not proven skilled and faithful in battle. A soldier does not walk in self-promotion, self-preoccupation, self-preservation, or self-appointment. A soldier waits on his commander, just as we must wait on our Commander, King Jesus.

As you find yourself tucked away in that hidden place, what are you waiting for? Are you waiting to be seen? Are you waiting to be heard? Are you waiting to be accepted and understood? Are you waiting to be rescued? Whatever it is you are waiting for will not be achieved through any of the tactics demonstrated by our friends in the story of *The Emperor's New Clothes.* If you choose to try them, you will discover them useless and destructive in the end. You and I must yield to the waiting process (see Psalm 27:14). We must embrace it as a weapon of humility and use it to fight every temptation and every trap that promises to bring temporary solutions to our problems (see Psalms 25:3; 39:7). All we require is available to us from the One who sees, hears, accepts, and understands (see Psalm 62:5). What needs to be revealed will be revealed in its season (see Habakkuk 2:3), and we will not lose anything of who we are and what we are destined to become by waiting. On the contrary, it is in waiting that our identity, our purpose, and the fulfillment of that purpose become more and more refined and more and more defined (see Joshua 23:14). We are to wait on the Lord just as Sarah did. He will not disappoint us. For with Him all things are possible (see Mark 10:27).

DISCUSSION QUESTIONS

1. Most of my life my greatest struggle has been…
   a. Wanting to be seen, but feeling invisible.
   b. Aching to be heard, but doubting anyone would listen.
   c. Desiring to be accepted, but thinking I had to be something I wasn't.
   d. Hoping to be understood, but unable to freely express myself.
   e. Other.

2. What are you waiting for?
   a. Promotion or advancement in a certain area of life?
   b. God's promises as you walk in His truths?
   c. The next set of marching orders?
   d. Other.

3. "With Him all things are possible." What are you believing for?

CHAPTER SEVEN

Weapon Five: Let the Lord Defend You

But let all those who take refuge and put their trust in You rejoice; let them ever sing and shout for joy, because You make a covering over them and defend them; let those also who love Your name be joyful in You and be in high spirits. Psalm 5:11

Too Good To Be True

What would you say if I told you that someone stands waiting and wanting to defend you every moment of your life, that your own personal champion stands eager to fight every battle with you? That there is someone keeping watch over you day and night making sure that you get what you need when you need it? That when trouble finds you, someone with the power to walk you through that trouble is on your side no matter how hopeless it might seem? That there is a voice from Heaven ready to speak on your behalf whenever necessary? What would you say? Would you say that you find it hard to believe anyone could care that much about you? Would you say that you understand all of this to be true in your head but find it difficult to believe in your heart? My friend, you are not alone. Many of us struggle with the idea of having our own personal Defender, Champion, Provider, and Protector. Why do we struggle? We struggle because it sounds too good to be true.

To believe that there is someone willing to defend us would be to admit that we are worth defending. To believe that there is someone desiring to watch over us would be to admit that there must be something special about us. To believe that there is someone able to meet all of our needs would be to admit that our needs are important. To believe that there is someone who is willing to speak out on our behalf is to admit that he cares for us unconditionally. For various reasons, many of us struggle with the fact that we are worth defending, that we are special, that our needs matter, or that someone loves us with no strings attached. We rationalize that there must be a catch. There must be some sort of hidden agenda. There must be some super-fine print somewhere explaining our part in this unbelievable contract. The truth is there is no catch. There is simply a God wanting us to believe because He loves us—no catch, no conditions, just love.

Unconditional love is something that is foreign to much of society today. How does the old saying go? "There is no such thing as a free lunch," implying that everything has a price and comes with conditions. For example, a father refuses to express his love for his son unless he does exactly what is expected. An employee holds back using special gifts and talents as a bargaining tool for a better position and a pay raise. A friend calls to "check up" on you, all the while intending to acquire some juicy information concerning the latest neighborhood scandal. Many people have learned to master the fine art of conditional relationship. They go after what they want by manipulating and controlling a situation, knowing that there will be some type of self-satisfaction, some sort of payoff. Unfortunately, they get the desired payoff while you pay the price. That may be true of some people you and I have dealt with in the past, but that is not true of Father God. He has already paid the price, thus removing any need for conditions. His love is a free gift that He has chosen to direct our way daily whether we choose to believe in it or not.

If you have a difficult time believing in God's unconditional love, all you have to do is ask and He will help you believe. If you believe in your head but doubt in your heart, ask Him to change your heart. If you do not doubt the love of God, there is a question I would like to ask you. At the first sign of trouble, when the darkness falls, when you are all alone and backed into a corner, whom do you seek to defend you? Do you rely on those around you to bring defense and relief? Do you tend to cry out, defending yourself? Or, do you seek the help of the One who loves you no matter what?

YOU TAKE CARE OF IT FOR ME...

In the midst of overwhelming problems it is natural for us to seek some kind of relief. Recognizing our need for help, we might seek someone we can trust, lay everything out on the table, and secretly expect them to hand over all the answers right then and there. Sometimes the answers will come from the wise counsel we seek, but not every time. There will be occasions when the answers to our particular problem are not available. After all, there is no one on earth who holds every answer to every question! When the answers we desperately seek do not come, we may easily become aggravated. Tormented by our troubles and desperate for reprieve, we grow frustrated with those from whom we originally sought help. Yet we are totally unaware of the potential consequences that frustration might bring. Before we know it, our frustration leads to anger, anger leads to a wrong attitude, and a wrong attitude leads to wrong actions. Eventually we find ourselves viewing those we previously trusted as lacking in cooperation and insight. Filled with pride, we begin to question their "spirituality" and "maturity" and resort to gossip and slander, resulting in an end that is more dreadful than the beginning. We discover that the overwhelming problem remains unsolved, a previously healthy relationship is injured, and a decent reputation is damaged, all because we looked to others to defend us and rescue us from the difficulties of life. Is it wrong of us to go to one another for counsel? Of course not! The Word instructs us to do so. But when we do, we must not expect more of our counselors than they are capable of giving.

I'LL TAKE CARE OF IT...

Another natural alternative in seeking relief and rescue is for us to step up, speak up, and be our own defenders.

Backed into a corner of some kind and fighting to be released, we recognize our need for rescue. We look around for help, only to find that there is none to be found. As far as we can see, no one is willing to speak or to act on our behalf and so we take on the challenge of helping ourselves. We speak out, boldly proclaiming our rights. And while it is healthy to understand the importance of personal boundaries, we were not designed to take matters into our own hands in every situation. Nor were we designed to place our focus totally on ourselves. We were created to place our focus on the One who made us and on those He has placed around us. To totally focus on self is called idolatry—placing our needs and wants above God. Once again, the end is more dreadful than the beginning. We discover that we have become lovers of self. We have isolated ourselves from the love and care of others and rejected the help of our divinely appointed Defender, Jesus.

In Genesis 38 we read the account of a woman by the name of Tamar who sought rescue and relief from a grim situation through self-defense. Not long after being chosen as the wife of Judah's firstborn, Er, Tamar found herself widowed. Er had greatly displeased God and was slain by Him. In obedience to the law, Judah went to his second son and told him to receive Tamar as his wife so that offspring would be born of them for the sake of his older brother. The second son, Onan, begrudgingly took Tamar as his wife. Not desiring to father any children who would not be considered his own, he took precautions to guarantee that Tamar did not conceive. This action displeased the Lord greatly, and the Lord slew Onan also. Left widowed and childless again, Tamar was promised the third son, Shelah, once he became of age. Until that time, Tamar was to live the life of a widow in her father's house. Obediently she left her home and returned to her father. There she lived waiting until Shelah was old enough to call for her, bringing honor to her name and fulfillment to her life. She waited and waited, but the call never came. It never came because Judah blamed

Tamar for the loss of his two older sons. Not wanting to lose his youngest, he conveniently forgot his promise to his daughter-in-law. As a result, Tamar found herself without a husband, without a child, without the support of her own father, without the respect of her father-in-law, and consequently without hope. Taking matters into her own hands, she did what she thought she needed to do. Masquerading as a harlot, she lured her newly widowed father-in-law into her bed through deceit and manipulation. Not long after, it was discovered that a child had been conceived.

Tamar took matters into her own hands, getting what she wanted, but at what cost? Yes, Judah had broken his promise. Yes, Tamar had been discarded. Yes, she needed rescuing and her honor needed defending. But not this way! This way dictated that she resort to lying, deceiving, and manipulating. This way demanded that she act in a way that was not only displeasing to God but also duplicated the very same mistakes made by her previous husbands that led to their deaths and to her current predicament. Tamar's overwhelming need to be exonerated had overpowered her.

THINGS BEGAN TO HAPPEN

Sarah had a similar experience to that of Tamar, and she too paid a great price. Frustrated and humiliated at the thought of being barren in a time when providing an heir for her husband was the most important thing a wife could do, Sarah took matters into her own hands. As a result of her providing a surrogate mate for her husband, a male child was born to carry on the family name and traditions. Unfortunately, this arrangement proved to be more than uncomfortable for all concerned. In addition to the discomfort, it was obvious that Sarah had gotten ahead of God's plan. Why did she do it? She did it because exoneration meant more to her than anything else at the time. Fortunately, God in His grace and mercy provided her with another opportunity to experience His divine defense.

Referring back to our main scripture passage in Genesis 12:11-20, we encounter Sarah placed in a position with little hope. Sarah in captivity to a foreign king for the purposes of his pleasure, could not speak on her own behalf. Her husband Abraham, in captivity to fear, would not speak on her behalf. What would become of her now that all available voices had been silenced? Who would come to her rescue, defending her honor and rewarding her obedience? The One who created her and sustained her up until now. He became her voice in her time of need. He fought for her release. He fought for her honor. He fought for her marriage. He fought for her promise. He spoke His words defending her and things began to happen.

He'll Take Care of It...

You and I do not have to be imprisoned by a foreign king and facing utter destruction in order to experience the need for a Defender. Just as there are many reasons for one to require the defense of a lawyer in a court of law, there are many reasons that call for the Defender, Jesus. The good news is that He stands ready and eager to fight for you and me whenever we need Him. He is the One who sees where we are and what we need. He is the One who will speak on our behalf when we cannot, or should not. He is the One who is our hope. Listen to the words of the psalmist in Psalm 121.

> *I will lift up my eyes to the hills* [around Jerusalem, to sacred Mount Zion and Mount Moriah]—*From whence shall my help come? My help comes from the Lord, Who made heaven and earth. He will not allow your foot to slip or to be moved; He Who keeps you will not slumber. Behold, He Who keeps Israel will neither slumber nor sleep. The Lord is your keeper; the Lord is your shade on your right hand* [the side not carrying a shield]. *The sun shall not smite you by day, nor the moon by night. The Lord will keep you from all evil; He*

will keep your life. The Lord will keep your going out and your coming in from this time forth and forever-more.

The psalmist knew where to look for help. He set his eyes on the things above, knowing that his help and his defense came from the Lord, who made all things. His heart was settled. He did not need to worry, because the Lord watched over him day and night. When the heat of life was turned up, his Lord would provide the shade. When the evil one sought to destroy him, his Lord would confuse his evil plan. When he went out, he was blessed. When he came in, he was blessed. What resolve and faith the psalmist was able to express!

Do you and I express such resolve as the psalmist? When the heat gets turned up in our lives, what do you and I do? Whom do we seek to defend us? Do we set our eyes upon Jesus or do we set our eyes on other people? Do we take matters into our own hands, making them worse than when we started? Do we put our hope in the One who created us and sustains us, or do we refuse His offer of defense? These are tough questions that you and I must be willing to answer.

To deny the divine defense of the Lord is to reveal our pride. It says that we prefer to take matters into our own hands, that His assistance is not necessary. My friend, such an attitude reveals one thing and one thing only: We lack humility and walk in pride. Humility says, "I need the Lord to defend me." Pride says, "I can handle it on my own." Pride hurts the very heart of God because it blocks the flow of His love in our lives. We were made for love, and He is love. Pride blocks love. That is not to say that God's love toward us weakens or becomes less, but that the act of pride positions us where we are unwilling to receive that love.

Do you want God's unconditional love to reach you? Do you want to believe in a God who stands ready to defend you and keep you and provide for you? Do you want to release all that you are and all that you will be to a Father who knows what is best for you? Do you long for a voice that will speak out for you when trouble comes? If so, then you must resist pride and humble yourself under the mighty hand of God (see 1 Peter 5:6). He will do the rest.

I Will Not Be Moved

Learning the use of this particular weapon of humility has proven to be a struggle for many in the Lord's Army. It takes much time and effort to master the use of the various tools in the arsenal. Yet this weapon lies untested, untried. Why? It sits untried because of the skills required to master its effectiveness. While other weapons call for varying degrees of patience and self-control, this weapon requires much more. It requires meekness. Meekness dictates a silenced tongue, and a silenced tongue comes from a totally surrendered life.

You and I sing the song "I Surrender All" with the full intention of doing just that, yet within a very short period of time we find ourselves engaged in the fight once again. The battle for control between what the flesh wants and what the Spirit wants is a battle we face each and every day. Some days the flesh appears to win, and other days the Spirit. Paul spoke of this in the eighth chapter of Romans, coming to the conclusion that our only hope of winning the battle between the law of the flesh (the law of sin and of death) and the law of the Spirit is through the power of the Spirit of life. It is by the empowerment of the Holy Spirit that our battle cry can become, "He is my defense; I will not be moved." Surrendering with hands lifted up to Him, we are called to relinquish all rights, allowing Him the pleasure of defending us and defeating our foe. That is His desire. That is His plan.

Things Will Begin To Happen

I can almost see you sitting there as Tamar did, battling not only the discouragement that threatens to overtake you, but also the overwhelming urge to exonerate yourself. After all, just as with Tamar, promises have been made and you have done everything you have been asked to do. But still your heart echoes her cry, "How much longer do I have to wait? Who will speak for me? When will the promises be fulfilled?" I assure you that there is only One who has the power to end the wait, there is only One who has the voice to triumph over the silence, and there is only One who has the desire to fulfill the promises: King Jesus.

My friend, taking matters into your own hands may cost you more than you have to give. Therefore, I encourage you to hold on, knowing that God will do what needs to be done when and how it needs to be done. As you wait upon Him, put on meekness and fight the daily battle with the weapons of humility, just as Abraham's Sarah fought. And like Sarah, you will discover that when you are found humbly expressing your need for the divine Defender, He will be moved: moved to defend you, moved to validate you, and moved to vindicate you as you put your faith in Him. He will become your voice in your time of need. He will fight for your release. He will fight for your honor. He will fight for your marriage. He will fight for your promise. He will speak His words in your defense and things will begin to happen.

What if you have already gone ahead of His plan? What if you have acted out of pride, operated in manipulation, and made matters worse? What do you do? You ask the Lord for forgiveness. Then you ask Him to extend His grace to you, allowing another opportunity to experience His divine defense. He did it for Sarah. He will do it for you. Remember, His love is unconditional.

I pray that, like the psalmist, you and I will know where to look for help. May we set our eyes on the things above, knowing that our help and our defense come from the Lord, who made all things. I pray that our hearts will be settled in that we need not worry, because the Lord watches over us day and night. As with the psalmist, when the heat of our life is turned up, our Lord will provide the shade. When the evil one seeks to destroy us, our Lord will confuse his evil plan. When we go out, we will be blessed. When we come in, we will be blessed. I pray that we will learn to freely express our resolve and our faith, rejoicing in the goodness of our personal Defender, Champion, Provider, and Protector.

Discussion Questions

1. The following best describes where I find myself today:

a. I have a difficult time believing that someone cares enough for me to be my personal Champion.

b. I believe in my personal Champion in my head, but I have yet to believe in my heart.

c. I believe.

2. It is a struggle for me to believe that...
   a. I am worth defending.
   b. I am special.
   c. My needs are important.
   d. Love can be unconditional.

3. Share a time when you went to another for counsel and did not receive what you expected to receive. How did you react?

4. Share a time when you chose to defend yourself, attempting to be released from a difficult situation. What price, if any, did you pay?

5. I admit that I can relate more to...
   a. Tamar and the need to manipulate the situation.
   b. Judah and his broken promise.
   c. Sarah and her silence.
   d. Abraham and his silence.

e. The psalmist and his ability to set his eyes on the things above.

6. If I were to cry out today, I would cry out to God to...
   a. Fight for my release.

b. Fight for my honor.

c. Fight for my marriage.

d. Fight for my promise.

e. Fight for things to begin to happen.

7. I am at a point where I need to ask the Lord to forgive me for getting ahead of His plan. True/False

CHAPTER EIGHT

Weapon Six: Look to the Lord for Validation and Vindication

*Vindicate me, O Lord, for I have walked in my integrity;
I have* [expectantly] *trusted in, leaned on, and relied on
the Lord without wavering and I shall not slide.*

Psalm 26:1

STEADY AS SHE GOES

In many places of business, team-building exercises have proven to be a successful means of improving communication skills and promoting cooperation and understanding among coworkers. One of my favorite team-building exercises is to ask people to describe themselves through the use of a visual. Each person is given a list of several different types of boats and asked to pick the one that best describes them. One chooses the tugboat, seeing herself as small but powerful when it comes to helping others along. Another chooses the tanker, viewing himself as one that is built for carrying heavy loads. One visualizes herself as a cruise ship always ready to take on more friends, promoting fun and friendship. Still another sees himself as a fast, sleek submarine surfacing only when absolutely necessary. Before long, each one in the group is able to identify with a specific kind of boat and point to it and its attributes for the purpose of sharing something about themselves with one another.

You and I could easily do the same thing. We could take a look at the list of boats and choose one that best describes us in order to explain to others something about the way we operate in the waters of life. By doing so we would be able to understand each other a little better. But you and I know that there is more to a boat than its general build, features, and purpose. There are also important components lying below the surface that we cannot easily see, such as the propeller that advances the boat and the anchor that stills it.

The rotation of the propeller creates the force that moves a boat forward or backward. By adjusting the speed of the propeller, the travel speed of the boat is also adjusted — fast to slow, slow to fast. There are times when a boat must go full speed ahead in open waters for the purpose of making good time and adhering to the assigned schedule. There are also times when the boat must slow down for safety and security so that it can maneuver in tight, difficult places. When the propeller stops, the boat stops.

As you and I imagine ourselves as boats in the waters of life, we might want to take the time to ask ourselves what it is that propels us. I can tell you that the list would be far too extensive to allow a thorough discussion. So we will draw two different entries from our "propeller possibility" list and briefly discuss each one. The two propellers I speak of work hand in hand. One establishes a declaration, while the other gives evidence to support the declaration. The first is called validation and the second vindication.

What does it mean to be valid? To be considered *valid* is to be "legitimate in existence: to be acceptable and genuine."[6] *Validity* is being "authentic in action or function: true, reliable, and faithful."[7] Something that is *valid* is deemed as "suitable for use: appropriate, fitting, proper and correct."[8] In essence, *validity* is the state of being "substantiated, supported, and confirmed."[9]

To be *vindicated* is to be "set free, delivered."[10] Vindication brings about exoneration and absolution, resulting in verification and justification. In essence, vindication is being defended against denial or censure.

Validation and vindication are life propellers. Who would not want to experience events in life where their existence was deemed legitimate? Who would not want their actions considered authentic? Who would not want to be seen as suitable to perform a task they know they can do? All of us possess a need and a desire to be substantiated, supported, and confirmed as we travel the waters of life.

Validation and vindication work in cooperation with one another. First, validation substantiates and confirms, and then vindication provides the evidence or proof. For example, a young person does well on a test. His teacher says to the student, "You have made great improvement. I can tell that you have applied yourself and studied hard." This declaration of praise no doubt substantiates the efforts of the hardworking student and gives him a sense of accomplishment. In addition to verbal support, the teacher provides evidence of her declaration by giving the student a high grade. The declaration validates the student's hard work, while a higher score provides the necessary evidence for vindication.

What do you think happened inside the student when his instructor recognized his effort, voiced his approval, and placed a better than passing grade on his test? Do you think he felt good about himself? Sure he did! Do you think this interaction might have given him incentive for the future? There is a great possibility! Do you think that because of this incentive, his desire to try harder could increase? You'd better believe it!

On the other hand, what would have happened if the interaction between the two had gone another way? What if the teacher did not say a word to her student? Maybe she felt that the student had been goofing off in the past and finally showed a little responsibility, but not enough to make a big deal about it. Maybe she was uncomfortable handing out compliments. Maybe she just didn't notice. Whatever the case, she would have missed a great opportunity to influence her student in a positive way. As a result, instead of being propelled forward, the student might easily be discouraged, stop trying, and fall farther behind.

Although this would be considered a counterproductive scenario brought about by the instructor, there is another twist to this story. You and I know that in a perfect world everyone would receive all the validation and vindication they needed. But we do not live in a perfect world. And just as our student did not receive the incentive he may have desired, we may not receive the incentive we desire. When this takes place—and it will—what will our response be? Will we give up and drop anchor? Or will we continue steadily moving forward?

To give up and drop anchor would be admitting that we must rely on other people to get us where we need to go. Is that truly the case? Does vindication and validation from our fellowman dictate the conditions of our voyage? No, because it is not man who decides how fast or slow the propeller rotates; it is God. He is the One who works by means of validation and vindication. He declares. He supports with evidence. He propels. He dictates. This tells you and me that if we feel validation and vindication is lacking in our lives, we are pronouncing that our God is falling down on the job!

You and I want to be steadily moving forward. With our anchors on deck and our propellers ready for action, we must rely totally on the Father as we patiently and expectantly wait for things to happen.

Sometime in the Night

What type of a boat do you envision Sarah as? Whatever the look, size, or potential speed of the seafaring vessel named "Sarah," it stood empty at the time in our current scripture study. Remember that Sarah was declared barren. She was unable to produce children, unable to achieve her one desire in life. If anyone was in need of validation and vindication, it was Abraham's Sarah. During this dark time in her life, she must have entertained many questions about her very existence.

She was empty and alone, going nowhere fast. It was as if she had been dry-docked, scrubbed down, painted, and set out to dry. Her obvious beauty had been recognized and validated. But her main reason for living, to conceive a child and mother a nation, lay unnoticed, unappreciated, and unfulfilled. Sarah found herself in waters almost too difficult to navigate. If it had not been for the love of her God and His desire to see her fulfilled in life, she would have spent the rest of her days empty and permanently anchored.

In her time of immobility and emptiness, God stepped in. He propelled her into the place she was always meant to be. He spoke in her defense, as we saw in the previous chapter, and things began to happen. It transpired sometime during the night while she lay sleeping. Her Defender spoke to her captor, revealed her true identity, and commanded her release. The very next day the words she longed to hear came from the man who had abducted her and considered her his very own. And in Genesis 20:16 we read,

> *And to Sarah he said, behold I have given this brother of yours a thousand pieces of silver; see, it is to compensate you* [for all that has occurred] *and to vindicate your honor before all who are with you; before all men you are cleared and compensated.*

King Abimelech not only returned Sarah to her husband, Abraham, declaring her his wife, but he also supported his declaration with a gift. Validation and vindication had come through the least expected one, initiated by the One most able and most willing. As a result, Sarah was returned to her rightful place and exonerated in front of all of mankind. What a story! What a testimony!

Sarah's vindication was a public event. Everyone within hearing distance knew of what God had done on her behalf. Imagine what it was like for her to go back to her people. No doubt there was celebration in the camp that very day. For Abraham and Sarah and everyone around them, this was an event to remember. It was the day that God spoke and things were set in motion.

Though Sarah's experience of vindication proved to be very public, that may not always be the case for you and me.

Validation and vindication take on many different forms. They may appear suddenly or gradually, publicly or privately, grandly or humbly. In no two cases is advancement of the propeller the same, because no two voyages are the same. Nevertheless, when the Father says it is time for one of His own to be substantiated, supported, and confirmed, there is no stopping Him. It will be done.

Keep in mind that the validation and vindication I speak of will always propel us to a place of trusting the Father more and serving His people better. It is never for the sake of personal gain or notoriety, but for the sake of glorifying God and advancing His Kingdom. Many people have mistaken substantiation and confirmation for a means of getting personal satisfaction and filling a void left inside from the loss or the absence of one thing or another. And though the void areas in each of us must be addressed and filled with the presence of God, it is not for the sake of personal satisfaction, but for the sake of becoming vessels that will withstand the waters of life. And until the void has been taken care of, it will ultimately exhaust every effort just to keep afloat.

Words Unspoken

Many precious people eventually discover themselves exhausted of all energy as a result of attempting to keep a damaged vessel afloat. For example, a young woman unexpectedly reunites with her father who divorced her mother and distanced himself from the entire family for many years. Doing the best she could, the mother raised all of her children to know that they were loved and accepted. The mother's love was never questioned by her eldest daughter, though she still longed for the day when she could hear words of love from the man who had abandoned her long before. The daughter grew up to be a fine young woman, seeming to have it all together on the outside, but nevertheless yearning for acceptance on the inside. To her father's credit, he never missed sending a card on her birthday or mailing a gift for Christmas. Unfortunately, he never gave her the one thing she desired most of all: his spoken declaration of love. One day she turned to take her three-year-old son into the grocery store and there stood her father. How did she know it was her father? She looked just like him. They stared at each other for a long time until he finally broke the ice. He told her how he had followed her throughout the years, watching her as she went to school and keeping an eye on her as she played with her friends at the park. He was there the day she graduated, and he stood across the street the day she walked out of the church holding the hand of her new husband. He had loved her more than she could ever have imagined, but he never told her until that day. The love this father had for his daughter was held captive in his heart, unexpressed, unreleased, unfulfilled until then. The love he had for her was always valid, but never proven. He ultimately realized that cards and gifts could never replace the loving words and the gentle touch of a father.

What do you think would have happened to this young woman if she had never run into her father? What if the words of love had never come? What would have become of her and the unwanted void in her life? She would have found herself faced with two choices. First, she could continue on with her life the best she knew how, just like her mother did. Left unattended, the void would continue to exist; plugged up and camouflaged, it would allow nothing and no one to enter it. As the void gradually grew, greater attempts to block the effects of the hidden barrenness would exhaust our friend and bring her to a point of despondency and despair. The only other alternative would be to acknowledge her need and seek help from the One who knew all about being abandoned, all about being separated from a father, and all about hungering for spoken love. She could go to Jesus. There she would find compassion, comfort, and a cure.

My friend, if you are relating to this young woman and recognizing that there is a void in your life needing repair, I want to encourage you by telling you that you are not alone. There is no need to hide. There is no need for guilt or shame. Every one of us has holes created by life situations that unceasingly threaten to sink us. How do we deal with them? Where do we go? We go to the Master Shipbuilder. He is standing by, waiting for you and me to make our requests for repair and restoration known. And when we do, He is ready to protect and preserve those vulnerable areas of our lives as He puts His hand to the task of making them better than new. He is the One who originally built us and He is the only One who can completely repair us (see Isaiah 58:12). If you are ready to reach out to Him, I entreat you to say this prayer with me:

Father God,

I need You. I need Your compassion, Your comfort, and Your cure. The situations of my life have left me in need of repair and I am afraid I will sink if You do not come to my rescue soon. I have looked to others as my source of validation and vindication and I have been disappointed time and time again. Now I see that I was wrong. Now I see that only You can give me what I need. You are my source of validation. You are my source of vindication. Only You can fill the empty places inside of me and propel me into the future You have planned.

I choose to release the disappointments. I choose to release my expectations of others. I choose to release all doubt and fear. And I ask You to do what needs to be done to repair those things in me that have been damaged. I want to be restored so that I might glorify You and be a vessel that will somehow be a small part of building Your Kingdom. I thank You for Your goodness and Your mercy that is new every morning (see Lamentations 3:22-23). I thank You for Your love that never fails. I thank You for Your faithfulness that has become my source of hope and my reason for joy. I release my life to You this day and every day that follows. I love You.

In the name of Jesus, I say this prayer.

VALIDATORS AND VINDICATORS

Our chapter would be incomplete if we did not take the time to discuss what it means to be one who validates and vindicates through the power of our God, for the glory of His name, and for the sake of others. We were commissioned by the apostle Paul, in Ephesians 5:16, to be "*making the very most of the time* [buying up each opportunity]" and, in Philippians 2:4, to "*Let each of you esteem and look upon and be concerned for…the interests of others.*"

When was the last time you and I took the initiative to recognize another, see the effort that they were making to overcome a challenge, and offer some incentive to propel them forward? When was the last time you and I sat down to send a card or letter reinforcing God's love to a friend, or even an enemy? When was the last time you and I set aside our interests for the interests of others?

We have been given the power from the Father and through the Spirit to propel others as they face the ever-changing waters of life. He has chosen us to be the incentive for those who are weary, the joy for those who fight sadness, and the words of love to those who hunger for acceptance. What a commission! What a responsibility! What a gift! But like many gifts that are opened yet never used, we may have regarded this gift in the same way. If that is the case, then we have been missing opportunities every day.

I encourage you, my friend, to allow the Lord to show you how to be a validator and a vindicator in His great army. To do so will require several actions on your part. The first requirement is to allow the Lord to make the necessary repairs to all damaged areas resulting from the past. The second is to ensure that your anchor is hoisted and placed securely on deck, indicating your readiness to move. The third is to make sure that your propellers are prepared to rotate. The fourth is to wait patiently on the Lord for direction. And the fifth requirement: Expect great things to happen!

DISCUSSION QUESTIONS

1. What boat best describes you? Explain
    a. Speedboat
    b. Rowboat
    c. Tugboat
    d. Sailboat
    e. Submarine
    f. Cruise ship
    g. Tanker
    h. Other _____

2. What would you say is the one thing that propels you the most?

3. Describe a time in your life when you hungered for validation and vindication.

4. Describe a time in your life when God granted you validation and vindication through another person.

5. Describe a time in you life when God allowed you the privilege of giving validation and vindication to another person.

6. What would it take for you to become more aware of the daily opportunities to validate and vindicate others?

7. At the present time I admit that I am...
    a. Taking on water and in desperate need of repair.
    b. Lifting up my anchor; getting ready to move.
    c. Preparing my propellers for action.
    d. Waiting on the Lord.
    e. Expecting great things.
    f. Other _____.

8. I have released others from any expectations I may have placed on them and choose to look to the Lord who decides when and how to work through His people for the purpose of propelling me.

_____

Signature

CHAPTER NINE

Weapon Seven: Let the Lord Reward Your Inheritance

The LORD recompense thy work and a full reward be given thee of the LORD God of Israel, under whose wings thou art come to trust.   Ruth 2:12(KJV)

A Grand Display

It was more than obvious by the periwinkle-blue sky and the graceful approach of the sun that a new day was dawning. The field of wheat sparkling from the early hour blanket of dew released an aroma promising to draw in anyone willing to stop and admire the full-grown harvest. The field extended as far as the eye could see. This breathtaking sight combined with the pleasant aroma evoked not only a feeling of warmth but also one of anticipation. On taking an even closer look, it seemed as if each stalk of wheat had its own unique appearance, its own personality. And in viewing the field as a whole, it was apparent that many of the stalks reflected the rays of the rising sun, creating a grand display of light. This was no ordinary field of wheat. This field was alive: alive with anticipation and excitement, alive with expectation and joy, alive with the knowledge that something was about to happen.

Jesus explained to His disciples, in Matthew 13:38-43, that:

> *The field is the world, and the good seed...the children of the kingdom...The harvest is the close and consummation of the age. The Son of Man will send forth His angels, and they will gather out of His kingdom all causes of offense....Then will the righteous (those who are upright and in right standing with God) shine forth like the sun*

in the kingdom of their Father. Let him who has ears [to hear] *be listening, and let him consider and perceive and understand by hearing.*

Jesus said that the world you and I live in is the Father's field—a field where He sows seed, tends to it daily, and personally oversees it as it grows. Though the enemy attempts to come in and inhibit the growth of the field, it is apparent that the crop from the good seed continues to grow and shine as the Father intended. The good seed is called, named, and marked as the children of the Kingdom of God and no invasion of bad seed can change that. Jesus said that the world as we know it will surely come to a close when He commands His angels to commence harvesting. The children of the evil one will be permanently removed, but the children of God's Kingdom, the righteous, will shine like the sun and remain with the Father forever. Eternity with the Father is our ultimate inheritance as His children, just as eternity with His people is the ultimate inheritance of our Lord Jesus. That is what is called a win-win situation!

When you and I, in faith and by God's grace, release our hearts and our lives to Him, we are born into a new Kingdom—the Kingdom of God the Father, God the Son, and God the Holy Spirit. Being born into this heavenly Kingdom immediately bestows privileges (an inheritance if you will) upon us that we could never have imagined. The first and most important of all privileges is the opportunity to remain in the presence of our heavenly Father forever. It is a future that you and I could not possibly imagine in our limited thinking; nevertheless, it awaits us.

Not only will you and I inherit the eternal presence of the Father in Heaven, if we know Him and love Him on earth, but we will also benefit from our actions. Each one will be rewarded accordingly. Jesus said, in Matthew 16:27(KJV), *"For the Son of man shall come in the glory of his Father with his angels; and then he shall reward every man according to his works."* I remember thinking when I first read these words that I had better get busy and do some good deeds and make a large deposit into my heavenly account. I wanted to make sure that there was enough to cover any unexpected withdrawals. Eventually I realized that though good deeds are necessary at the appropriate times and places, that is not the concept to which this scripture refers. It refers to the choices we make. In other words, when opportunity approaches, what is our response? Do we respond according to God's Word, or do we have a different response? The right response at the right time increases our inheritance, or treasures in Heaven, while the wrong response results in negative consequences meriting no increase at all.

Also adding to the treasures that you and I are building in heavenly places is our response to the call to become more like Jesus, who is the expression of the Father. For example, the Father found it of the utmost importance to sow seed and grow the harvest called man. Jesus spent His life on earth tending that seed which raises the questions, "Are we tending the seed God has planted? Are we promoting the growth of His harvest?" If we want to be like the Son, reflecting the Father, we must learn to become a people who have a heart for tending the souls of man for the sake of the Lord's harvest, His beloved Kingdom.

It is our relationship with the Father, the responses and choices we make with what we are given, and the time we spend tending the lives of others that determine the extent of our inheritance. The apostle Paul knew how to tend the growing harvest. He took all that he had and all that he had learned from the experiences of his life and poured it out over all those willing to receive. How did he do it? He spoke. He wrote. He traveled and visited. He shared what he loved the most—the truth about his God. He shared passionately and intently to the point where he freely admitted to his faithful friend Timothy, *"For I am already about to be sacrificed* [my life is to be poured out as a drink offering] (2 Timothy 4:6). The vessel called "Paul" may have been depleted, but the promise of an incredible harvest of souls was undoubtedly ensured.

In the parable of the lost son, in Luke 15:11-32, we discover an example of a young man who had not yet grasped the idea of depositing into heavenly treasures. At his request his father handed over his earthly inheritance before it was traditionally time to do so. The father, whether intentionally or not, was about to allow his son to learn a most valuable life lesson. Taking what was freely given to him, he proceeded to make all the wrong choices. Continuing his downward spiral until nothing remained; the young man reached the end of himself with no money, no food, no friends, and no pride. Eventually the young man returned to his father with nothing to offer but his experience. He had gone out with his pockets filled with money and his heart filled with pride. He returned with his stomach empty and his heart broken and humbled.

The choices we make determine the treasures we build. And though this young man made many wrong choices, his father never rejected him. On the contrary, he received him back into his house and bestowed upon him the finest food, clothing, and celebration possible. Why? He did it because he loved him. And in that pure and simple love of a father for his child, he was able to forgive the past by rejoicing in the present and looking forward to the future.

Maybe you have a past you would like to forget. Maybe you have a history filled with bad choices. I did. And yet when I made the choice to come back to the heavenly Father's arms, He bestowed upon me the best He had to offer. He did it for me; He will do it for you. No matter what mistakes you have made in the past, there is always forgiveness in His heart and room in His house for one more. If you find yourself in a position of needing a father and a home where love is pure and celebration is always in the air, the Father invites you to come home. And when you do, you will discover that there is a treasure chest waiting to hold all the treasures you will store up in the future by making godly choices. It is never too late!

There is no more rewarding way to build treasures in Heaven than to impact the treasures God has placed here on earth. Every treasure, every stalk of wheat, every person is unique with a personality all its own. Each and every one has been invited to be a part of the Kingdom. But not everyone has heard and understood this divine invitation. That is why you and I are here—to express and explain the invitation of God's love and to help those whom God values above all else become all that they can be for Him and for His glory. That is my assignment. That is your assignment. The Lord provides the seed, the soil, the sun, and the rain. You and I work the field with Him. As a result, each soul harvested by the work of our hands will receive an inheritance of their own.

WHEN YOU LEAST EXPECT IT

It is imperative for each of us to understand that the process of sowing and reaping takes time. A farmer does not go out into his fields the day after he plants his crop, expecting to see that it has become full-grown overnight. That is not the way it works. First, a seed is sown. Then it must fight against the weight of the soil to reach the air. Once it pushes through the resistance of the heavy soil into the air, it is ready to feed on not only the soil but also the sun and the rain. Growing is not its only chore. In addition to the growth process, the plant must also fight heavy winds, floods, drought, and insects. In spite of all that works against it, eventually a healthy plant reaches its full potential. All of this takes time.

As we begin partnering with the Father as workers in His field, we will undoubtedly face times of discouragement, frustration, and even exhaustion. It is all a part of the process. At times you and I might begin to question, "Why put forth so much effort when no results are visible?" These are the times the apostle Paul wrote about when he said, in Galatians 6:9, *And let us not lose heart and grow weary and faint in acting nobly and doing right, for in due time and at the appointed season we shall reap, if we do not loosen and relax our courage and faint.*

To see the harvest in its fullness will take energy, endurance, and courage on our part. To see the fullness of the inheritance in the Lord will take eternity. The good news is that we do not have to wait until we get to Heaven to begin receiving it. As we continue to grow in Him here on earth, a portion of our inheritance will gradually unfold and manifest by His hand in many different forms. You and I call them blessings: unexpected delights reminding us of His love, unanticipated strengths demonstrating His power, and unmerited favor expressing His mercy. In addition to the blessings He sends our way, our Father is also One who believes in rewarding His children. And though you and I should never expect rewards for the things that we do unto Him, we can expect our Father to be a Rewarder when we least expect it.

Harvest Delight

Abraham and Sarah made wrong choices just like our young man in the parable of the lost son. They chose to take what was given them—each other—and lie about their relationship for the sake of survival. Yet in spite of their actions which revealed a temporary lack of faith, their heavenly Father had a plan of rescue even before the choice presented itself. In His love, His power, and His mercy He chose to reward Sarah's humbling situation. He expressed His mercy by implementing His plan for her escape, knowing that Abraham and Sarah would find themselves in a precarious position with no way out. In His love for them, He chose to forgive their weaknesses and infuse strength into the situation. Demonstrating His awesome power, He evoked a reverent fear in the heart of the heathen king who held Sarah captive. As a result, the king not only returned her to her husband, but also gave them a portion of his wealth and a secure place to live in his kingdom. That is what I call a blessing! But that is not the end of it. After God's expression of mercy and demonstration of power, He chose to do one more thing for Sarah. He chose to remind her of His unfailing love by granting her the one desire that would genuinely delight her heart. He gave her a son.

Yes, she had been rescued and released from her personal prison. Yes, she had been returned to her rightful place. Yes, she had been reunited with her loved ones. Yes, she had not only been forgiven but also exonerated. But the fact remained that in spite of it all she was still barren, without offspring, left without a harvest of her own. Little did she know that through the use of the weapons of humility, Sarah was to become the recipient of the one treasure she had lost hope of ever possessing—a child. In the end, we discover that the promised child spoken of years before was awarded to Abraham and Sarah, not because of who they were, but because of who God is: the Sower, the Reaper, the Preparer, the Repairer, and the Rewarder of His people.

THERE IS ALWAYS A WAY OUT

Recently, I went home to visit my family. Sometime during the night, in the middle of my stay, a tire went flat on my car. Though it did not come as a complete surprise, since the tires were the originals and had endured a lot of mileage, it was definitely an inconvenience I could easily have done without. Knowing my dilemma, my parents blessed me by providing the solution. They had already planned to give my sisters and me a portion of our family inheritance. This blessing permitted me to purchase the tires I needed and helped ensure that my trip back home would be a safe and secure one.

That is how our heavenly Father works. He has prepared a personal life journey for each of us that will ultimately bring fullness, fruitfulness, and fulfillment, and glorify Him in the process. But sometimes, unexpected inconveniences happen. We get a flat tire. We run out of gas. We lose our direction and take the wrong road. But these little road-blocks do not fluster the Father at all. He already has the provision for the road before we need it. He has a storehouse of blessings ready to pour out on us when trouble arises. These blessings are just a portion of what is to come to those who identify with Him and love Him. They are provided so that we might continue our journey in security and safety. In other words, God's blessings are like a new set of tires for the road ahead. He provides them because He loves us and wants to see us move toward the goal He has lovingly and personally set.

There will be times when the roadblocks ahead appear impossible to overcome, resulting in fear and doubt and inviting the temptation to quit. When we encounter a roadblock and choose to stop, we are allowing the inconveniences to determine our future. If you or I had a flat tire, we would fix it. If we ran out of gas, we would fill up the tank. If we took a wrong turn, we would correct the error and move on. My friend, inconvenience is a delay, not a license to terminate the journey. For all we know, a flat tire might mean a divine delay protecting us from harm, an empty tank might permit a heavenly encounter allowing us the opportunity to bless another, and a wrong turn might provide an important life lesson we could draw on in the future. We must allow the Lord to provide the needs as roadblocks arise, knowing that He has our best interests at heart. He expects us to look to Him when the unexpected comes, knowing He will provide. He desires to see us moving toward the goal, not sitting on the side of the road. Sitting on the side of the road gets us nowhere fast, while moving steadily forward ensures that we will finish the journey and collect the prize—our inheritance in Him.

With this in mind, my friend, I would like to encourage you. No matter what roadblock has been set before you; there is a way out. For Sarah, there was a way out for her and her husband. For Moses, there was a way out for him and his enslaved people. For Esther, there was a way out for her and those she dearly loved. For Joseph, there was a way out for him and the kingdom he was born to serve by leading.

For Mary, there was a way out for her and her crucified Son. For you—no matter where you are, no matter what you have done, no matter what has been done to you—there is a way out. Do not let your past determine your future. Do not let the unexpected keep you from moving on and reaching the goal God has set before you.

The apostle Paul said, in Philippians 3:14 and 17,

> *I press on toward the goal to win the* [supreme and heavenly] *prize to which God in Christ Jesus is calling us upward....Brethren, together follow my example and observe those who live after the pattern we have set for you.*

And in Philippians 3:20, he said,

> *But we are citizens of the state (commonwealth, homeland) which is in heaven, and from it also we earnestly and patiently await* [the coming of] *the Lord Jesus Christ (the Messiah)* [as] *Savior.*

Paul warned us that to reach the goal set before us we would have to press on. This warning tells us that there will undoubtedly be some resistance along the way. Sometimes the resistance will be evident, sometimes not. Along with the encouragement to press on, Paul also implies that the prize awaiting us and calling us upward is worth hanging in there to obtain. In other words, we are to set our hearts on the goal, and, no matter what it takes, press on! How do we press on? Paul says one way is to observe others in the faith and follow their example. We are to follow them as they follow Christ. But in order to do such a thing we must use wisdom. Not everyone who claims to know Christ actually does. The best way to approach Paul's advice is to pray for the Lord to reveal someone who would exemplify the kind of person He wants you to be and then wait for His reply. Once you believe He has revealed His choice, begin to observe and test the fruit that lies behind the actions of your candidate (see Matthew 7:16). If the fruit is good, then watch them, learn from them, and follow them as they follow Jesus.

Along with the advice to follow those who are following Christ, Paul admonishes us to await the coming of the Lord earnestly and patiently. The coming he speaks of is the day of the Lord's return, when all will be made right under His mighty power. It is the day when He will command his angels to commence harvesting. The children of the evil one will be permanently removed, but the children of God's Kingdom, the righteous, will shine like the sun and remain with the Father forever. This is the inheritance He has chosen to award. It is our hope and our ultimate heart's desire. And in this hope we live with anticipation and excitement, with expectation and joy, with the knowledge that something is about to happen.

In Revelation 22:12(KJV), Jesus tells us, *"And, behold, I come quickly; and my reward is with me, to give every man according as his work shall be."* We do not know the day or the hour, but we do know the faithful One who made the promise. And in that promise, we stand waiting and anticipating the glory that is to come. As we wait for that glorious day, may we be a pleasant aroma, reflect the rays of the Father, enticing those willing to stop, admire, and join in the work of the field.

DISCUSSION QUESTIONS

1. What one word describes your feelings when you think about the fact that you could live in the presence of the Almighty God forever?

2. I am...
   a. Actively working in the Father's field.
   b. Not actively working in the Father's field.
   c. Trying to determine the best place for me to work in the Father's field.
   d. In need of rest from working in the Father's field.
   e. Other.

Explain

3. I currently find myself...
   a. At home and celebrating with the Father.
   b. Away from home needing the Father.
   c. Praying for another that is in need of the Father.
   d. Other.

Explain

4. The best way to describe the roadblock I currently face is_____.

5. When it comes to pressing on I'm like...
   a. A Mack truck
   b. A passenger car.
   c. A motorcycle.
   d. A pedestrian.
   e. Other.

Explain

6. When I think of Jesus coming back for me, the first thing that comes to mind is _____.

7. Knowing that my actions will impact my inheritance in heaven makes me want to _____ more often.

8. One way I can take a step toward impacting the harvest of souls is to _____ .

CHAPTER TEN

Wrapped Up In The Glorious Rhythm

*...I press on to lay hold of (grasp) and make my own,
that for which Christ Jesus (the Messiah) has laid hold of
me and made me His own.*   Philippians 3:12b

THE UNPREDICTABLE

Winter...Spring...Summer...Fall, Winter...Spring...
Summer...Fall, Winter...Spring...Summer...Fall, Winter...
Spring...Summer...Fall...

Living in Ohio as a child, I recall the four seasons being
more or less predictable, with each one lasting approximate-
ly three months. We knew from past experience that even
though the thermometer read ten degrees below zero on
any given day, the temperature would surely rise and usher
in the rains and the winds, resulting in opened windows,
beds filled with flowers, and longer, warmer evenings spent
swinging on the front porch. We also knew from experience
that the days of ninety-five to one hundred degrees were not
endless and that relief would gradually ease its way around
the corner. This welcomed relief brought with it days of
learning in school, nights of watching a new season of television shows, and weekends of jumping into freshly raked
mounds of fallen leaves. Life in Ohio with its four seasons
had a predictable pattern promising a safe, familiar flow.

Would it be fair to say that you and I would prefer most
things in life to be on the predictable side? Maybe it would
be more appropriate to say that we would most likely welcome information about the future more readily than we
might welcome surprises. Surely it would be less stressful
for us to see what lies around the corner so we could plan
for its approach. And you and I would sigh with relief
to know that when the heat was on, reprieve was soon to

follow. We dislike being uncomfortable. If discomfort must come, we want to know how long we will have to endure it. We dislike being left in the dark, and if darkness must come we want to know how long it will be before the light is turned on. There is no shame in the fact that you and I would prefer most things in life to be on the predictable side. It is the way we are wired.

But, in spite of our preferences, life allows very little room for predictability and comfort—even in the life of a believer. The pattern of the Christian life is void of the predictable, yet filled with faith. It is a life promising surprises all along the way, wrapped up in a glorious rhythm that far surpasses that of the predictable. In other words, those things we can easily see, calculate, and believe cannot compare with what awaits those who believe without seeing. Believing in the great goodness and the perfect timing of our God is what carries us through the seasons of this life of faith. And although the seasons designed by God cannot be predetermined or explained away, He has chosen to reveal a level of understanding concerning them so that we might gain all that is made available to us for the sake of knowing Him.

DISCERNING THE SEASON

Seasons in the spirit are unlike the seasons we are familiar with in the natural. They do not come in any special order but come when God's plan deems them necessary. They do not last a specific amount of time but last as long as needed. They do not always produce something that can be seen, but they produce nevertheless. The seasons in the natural have a repetitive flow, while the seasons in the spirit have a continuous flow that produces results building one upon the other. In spite of the fact that you and I are unable to rely on seasons extending for a set amount of time and always presenting themselves in the same order, we can rely on the fact that the Father is building something in our lives. And as He builds, He invites us to partner with Him as He daily unfolds and defines the attributes of whatever season we currently find ourselves in.

Defining the Season

A season in the spirit could be generally defined as a starting point, a pivotal point, or an ending point. A starting point could imply something new with the probability of training or maybe a new way of understanding something old. A pivotal point might be a time of extreme caution or a redirection of focus. A time of reflection and release would be more of an ending point.

Defining a season, even in the most general of terms, can tell us where we stand and how we are to proceed. When faced with something that is new (for example, a new hometown, a new job, a new ministry, or a new challenge), we would hopefully proceed with an open mind and a teachable spirit. We would want to proceed cautiously and thoughtfully when facing a life-changing decision that may demand a turnabout in our thinking or in our actions. When you and I find ourselves at a time when doors seem to be closing in areas of our lives, we hopefully would be willing to let go if and when necessary.

Acquainting ourselves with the seasons of the believer's life will deepen our understanding, help determine our direction, and build our faith. There are several steps we can take in order to acquaint ourselves with these seasons: (1) We must acknowledge that seasons in the walk of a believer actually exist. (2) We must allow the Father to introduce each season as He deems appropriate. (3) We must become students of the seasons and learn the attributes of each one. (4) We must discover the challenges and benefits of each. (5) And finally, we must learn to rely on the lessons taught in previous seasons to determine how to handle ourselves when faced with similar ones in the future.

Living out the Season

Once we are able to discern and define a season in the spirit, you and I need to know how to live it out. The seasons of the spirit do not last for any particular set time; each season lasts as long as needed in order to produce the desired results. The reality is that most seasons last longer than we would like or expect. There is a good chance that we will be "finished" with a season long before it is "finished" with us. When we reach that point, you and I are faced with a decision. We can stay where we are and allow the process to reach completion, yielding its fruit, or we can short-circuit the season and abort the process altogether.

Many a season has been short-circuited when the desire for comfort overruled the need for change and, instead of moving on, we settled for less. Impatience is another enemy of the season when it produces an impetuous zeal that insists on taking the lead and eventually gets ahead of the plan. Either way, short-circuiting any season will only halt the building process. And there is nothing more disheartening than to see a building unfinished, vacant, and unproductive. If it stays in this position for too long, the grass grows around it and it becomes an eyesore and an obstruction to those who are attempting to move past it. Is that what you and I aspire to be? No, of course not. We want to be built to completion with a specific purpose in mind. We want to be a help to others, not a hindrance. But most of all, we want to be pleasing to look at as we reflect the love of the Father.

If you have come to the conclusion while reading this chapter that you may have short-circuited the building process in your life, it is time to allow it to commence once again. The Father longs to see you complete and waits for your decision. I encourage you to take the time right now to express your desires to Him. He will be more than delighted to clear away the rubble and start building again right where He left off. He will see to it that you are completed with a purpose in mind, that you reflect His love, and that you become less of a hindrance and more of a help to those around you.

To live out the seasons of the spirit we must allow the Lord to build us and train us in the art of completion. Every season must reach its fullness. Why? Reaching fullness precedes closure, and closure heralds a new season. Living the believer's life is like walking down a hallway lined with doors. Just as it is only possible to enter one door at a time, it is only possible to live out one season at a time. Once a season is closed, a time of transition will take us to another.

Completing a season in the spirit will take resolve, determination, and sacrifice on our part and will no doubt invite resistance on the part of the enemy. It is his desire to see us short-circuit by settling or by rushing, and he will do all that is in his power to tempt us to do so. He knows that to abort a season is to hinder the growing process and hold us back from glorifying God. Beware of the temptation that sits at the door constantly, steadily knocking, waiting for an invitation to come in and take over. Giving in to temptation ends in abortion; giving in to the season generates hope, increases faith, and builds character.

Letting go of the Season

Short-circuiting a season is not the only temptation you and I will face as we do our best to live out our seasons. There is another temptation that is just as strong, if not stronger. It is the temptation to stay in the season after it is over. Why do we have such a problem letting go? We like the familiar. And when we become familiar with a situation, a location, or a season, we want to cling to it. We cling to it out of fear of the unknown. As a result, fear clings to us, which leads to a paralysis that keeps us from taking chances and moving out in faith. We also choose to hang on to what we know, even if it is over and done with, out of complacency. It is easier to stay in a dead place than to make the effort and sacrifice to leave and move into a new and living place. The problem with clinging is that it occupies our hands, keeping them from being able to reach out and take hold of what is waiting for us. When we cling to the past, we relinquish our future. We are saying to the One who created us and designed a plan for our lives that comfort is more important to us than He is.

If we are to take hold of all that is planned for our future for the sake of being complete and glorifying God, you and I must learn how to let go. We must learn to let go of seasons, let go of fear, let go of comfort, let go of people, places, and things. Letting go includes recognizing the signs of closure, releasing the past, allowing ourselves time to grieve, and opening our hearts to the future. When we begin a project, it has a beginning, a middle, and an end. We can tell that the end is approaching just by looking at the signs. So it is with a season of the spirit. And although the signs may not be visible to the human eye, the spirit can detect them. For example, when a season is coming to a close, those things that seemed to come easily will become more difficult. The reason for this is that the blessing, the anointing of God, for that season is being taken away. Or maybe there is a sense of dissatisfaction where satisfaction used to be. The doors of opportunity are closing and there seems to be little if any movement at all. All of these are possible signs of a season coming to an end. When we begin to sense signs such as these, it is time to go to the Father in prayer and ask for His divine explanation and direction.

Once the signs are clear and God is prompting us to take measures to begin releasing those things to which we have become accustomed, we must prepare our hearts and our minds for the process of letting go. How do we do it? First and foremost, we ask the Father for the grace to proceed. Second, we see the season as it is, not as it was. We accept the fact that it is a part of the past and that it does not belong to the future. We dedicate it to the Father, dig a hole, and then bury it. No matter what the season held for us in the past, letting go of it will always mean change. And change defined is death to what was and life to what is to be.

Death requires a time of grieving. When a season is over, we must allow ourselves the time to mourn. Mourning helps us to put all that has happened into perspective and gives us the freedom to express our feelings about our loss. Mourning is the hallway to the next door, the next season. The extent, type, and timing of mourning will be different for each person, for each situation. We need not compare ourselves with others when it comes to what it takes for us to settle with our own personal losses.

Once the burial has taken place and the time of mourning approaches its end, there is one more step to take. It is the step that will not only promote healing, but also invite vision for the future. It is the act of opening the heart to whatever lies ahead. To open one's heart takes faith, courage, and a willingness to change. It is never an easy task.

A NEW SEASON

The seasons in Sarah's life encapsulated in our main scripture of study are a prime example of living out and letting go. Sarah, accustomed to a life of love and security with her husband, Abraham, suddenly found herself apprehended and left in the hands of another man. In one day, her life turned upside down, landing her in an unimaginable place. A season had ended and a new one had begun. And from her perspective, this could have been where she would live out the rest of her days. Sarah had every reason to grieve and mourn her great loss. We do not know how long she stayed in this predicament, but we do know it was long enough for the people holding her in captivity to realize that their women were unable to conceive (see Genesis 20:17-18). This forced season of barrenness was God's reaction to what was taking place. I can- not help but believe that the Father was making a statement to the effect that if Sarah could not bring forth fruit, neither could anyone else. Nevertheless, this time of seclusion came to an end when Sarah was released and reunited with her husband. Yes, a season had ended and a new one had begun. It was a season of intimacy, a season of conception, and a season of fruitfulness. As a result, Isaac was born to Abraham and Sarah, ushering in yet another season, the season of parenthood. God's promise to Abraham and Sarah had finally come to its fullness, not in spite of the seasons they endured, but because of them.

You and I are also the fruit of Abraham and Sarah. We are children of the Kingdom that the Father brought forth when He commanded Abraham to leave all to go to a place he did not know. We are Kingdom kids. And Kingdom kids go through times of testing and growth just as Abraham and Sarah did. Those times are called seasons. There are seasons of rest and seasons of hard work, seasons of dry wilderness and seasons of rain. Seasons of transition and seasons of settling in. Seasons of doors opening and seasons of doors closing. Seasons of separation and seasons of connecting. Seasons of pressing on and seasons of holding back. Seasons of barrenness and seasons of fruitfulness. Seasons of apprehending and seasons of releasing. Seasons of doubt and seasons of security. Seasons of sowing and seasons of reaping. Seasons of receiving and seasons of distributing. Seasons of being exposed and seasons of being hidden, just to list a few.

Whatever season you and I might find ourselves in today, we can be sure that the Father sees us and knows just what it will take to live it out, and when necessary, let it go. He will reveal just enough about it to help us understand how to proceed. He will unfold His desires daily in order for us to receive all that He has made available. He will close doors. He will open doors. He will produce fruit in us that will live on long after we have left this earth.

I encourage you today to press on. Let nothing keep you from apprehending all that there is for you during this season of your life in the Lord. Take each day as it unfolds and allow yourself to be guided by the hand of the Father as He gives grace for the day. Settle in your heart that this season is necessary and that it too will pass when it is finished. Press on, whether it takes ten days, ten weeks, ten months, or ten years. Press on, whether you are surrounded by many or few. Press on, whether you see the results or not. Press on, allowing yourself to be built by the Father for the sake of bringing glory to Him. Press on, expecting a harvest of fruit. Press on, safe, secure, and all wrapped up in the glorious rhythm.

Discussion Questions

1. I prefer life when it is…
   a. Predictable.   b. Unpredictable.
   c. Constantly changing. d. Unchanging.
   e. Other.

2. When it feels like the heat has been turned up in my life, I tend to_____.

3. When it feels like I am surrounded by darkness, I tend to_
   _____.

4. The season I find myself currently living could be generally defined as a…
   a. Starting point.   b. Pivotal point.   c. Ending point.

   Explain

5. When it comes to the seasons of a believer's life, I believe I struggle most with…
   a. Discerning.   b. Living out.   c. Letting go.

   Explain

6. It has become clear to me that…
   a. I have allowed fear to keep me from moving forward.
   b. I have settled, allowing complacency to determine my future.
   c. I have been stuck in the letting-go process and it is time to mourn and release the past.
   d. I have closed my heart to the future.
   e. I am presently learning how to discern, live out, and let go.
   f. Other.

7. The season I find myself currently in is best described as
   _____.

8. My prayer to the Father concerning the seasons of my life as a Kingdom kid is_____.

CHAPTER ELEVEN

Impossible To Miss

Many plans are in a man's mind, but it is the Lord's purpose for him that will stand.   Proverbs 19:21

ETERNAL LEGACIES

The time approaches. It is the time when everyone possessing a heart inclined toward loving the Lord and anticipating His appearance will be accounted for, sealed, and saved. They will be saved from eternal separation from God and the torture resulting from that separation. They will be saved from the grasp of the enemy and from sharing in his final destiny. When Jesus returns in all of His glory, it will be for a full and complete harvest of souls. It was the plan long before you and I came on the scene and it remains the plan today. Jesus Himself said, *"Sky and earth will pass away"* (Matthew 24:35). Many have tried to wish it away, explain it away, and even ignore it away. Their efforts will someday soon prove meaningless and fruitless. We do not know the day or the hour (see Matthew 24:36). All we know is that it will come. And when it does, you and I want to be ready.

We must not only see to it that we are ready for the Lord's appearing, but we are also called to assist others in doing so. We are called to work the harvest (see Matthew 9:38). We are to partner with the Lord as He prepares His people for His return. Working the field can prove to be rewarding, yet challenging at the same time. Why challenging? Because tending the field of this earth is more than farming know-how and agricultural techniques. It requires additional skills that are needed for the purpose of protecting the fields. It requires the skills of spiritual battle. The war for souls rages on in battles that we face daily. Some days it looks as if we are winning—some days it looks as if we are not.

Daily we work the fields. Daily we fight the enemy. Daily we resist the temptation to give in and give up as we rely on the strength that comes from above to maintain balance in a world that promotes every type of thing that would take us off balance. Living the life of a believer is hard work, yet it is the most rewarding and fulfilling life you and I could live. It promises hope when situations look hopeless, it provides grace when things become humanly unbearable, it reaps rewards from the seeds we diligently sow, it enlarges faith when we cannot see ahead, and it builds the lives of those around us. And yet none of these can compare with the joy we receive as we commune with our Lord and Savior, Jesus.

You and I are fighting the good fight. We are soldiers in the Lord's Army. And just as in any battle, there will be times of watching for signs, waiting for things to change, and being filled with the faith it will take to carry us through. No matter where we find ourselves today, we can be assured that we will be called upon to make a difference by stepping up, stepping out, and fighting when the Lord gives His command. And as we wait on Him, we must allow Him to take us into seasons that will prepare us for the task ahead. One of those seasons is the season of hiddenness. It is a place where we may find ourselves entertaining thoughts such as, "How did I get here? Is this all there is? Maybe I've missed it? Am I expecting too much?" It is a place where the Father is trying to get our attention through a time of testing and training. It is a place where we find ourselves held in a concealed and private spot, tucked away by His design.

In his time of testing, Moses learned how to lead multitudes from captivity to freedom. Trained in the art of submission, Esther honored those in authority and became God's mouthpiece to a king. Joseph, abused and concealed, chose to forgive his abusers, made the most of a difficult situation, and prepared the way for his family. Tucked away in a private place, Mary became the carrier of the greatest treasure known to man: Jesus. Each endured a time of hiddenness for the sake of being prepared, purified, promoted, and proven. Each experienced the plan of God in their life. And as a result, each made a significant difference.

Abraham and Sarah also found themselves in a dark place separated from each other, doubtful of their future, and dysfunctional in their approach. But this was no surprise to their God. He chose to use this place of helplessness and hopelessness to propel them into a deeper walk with Him. It was also during this time that Sarah was introduced to the weapons of humility that saw her through her predicament. In her confusion, she let the Lord define who she was and what she was called to do. In her captivity, she learned how to submit to those in authority over her. In her confinement, she learned how to serve all people with kindness. In her time of concealment, she waited on the Lord to reveal her true identity to all. In her weakness, she let the Lord defend her. In her worthlessness, she looked to the Lord for validation. In her humiliation, she looked to the Lord for vindication. In her moments of hopelessness and lack, she let the Lord provide.

Sarah was forced to look deep down inside for the answers to the many questions that plagued her mind. She would discover what had become her heart motivation. She would come face-to-face with the possibility that she had placed her hope in the wrong things. She would be forced to define her desired destination. Finally, the internal battle she diligently fought was won the moment she looked to her Heavenly Father, believing in His "Love Letter" to her. She now knew that the words He had spoken over her were life and truth. She now believed that the actions He had executed on her behalf were rooted in love. She now accepted the title He had given her, revealing who she was in His eyes. To her God she was full of potential and pregnant with promise. And from that day forward He would rule her heart, He would be her source of hope, and He would be her way home.

Coming into agreement with her Father in Heaven that day not only brought peace and hope to Sarah, it also brought a strength that she would learn to lean on again and again as the battles continued. It was her reliance on the love of the Father and the security of knowing who she was in Him that allowed her to fight the next battle with strength and honor. It was the battle of adhering to the law of the land and submitting to those who held authority over her. It was a battle that would go against the very values she held close. Realizing that she was powerless and that her life was on the line, she submitted to the authorities and found herself waiting and hoping for rescue.

With her hands tied and her heart broken, Sarah was left with no other work to do but to be an example for those around her. It would be safe to presume that Sarah was not the only woman held captive for the pleasure of the king. History tells us that there were many more. With that in mind, Sarah would have had many opportunities to help by serving others. They too would need hope. They too would need comfort. They too would need someone to relieve the sting of captivity and the pain of loss. Sarah unknowingly had been positioned in an environment where her natural instincts to mother could be developed and freely expressed. It was a mother-in-training's dream wrapped up in what seemed to be a nightmare. Rising to the occasion, Sarah had the opportunity to become a dispenser of love, to meet needs, and to make a difference.

In spite of the ample opportunities for ministry to others, Sarah's daily battles continued. Feeling invisible, having no voice, recognizing rejection, being mishandled, and being misunderstood undoubtedly took a toll on her body, soul, and spirit. To be treated in such a manner is to be *oppressed*, to be "troubled in the mind; worried; weighed down."[11] To be *oppressed* is to be "kept down by the cruel use of power."[12] Oppression is in complete opposition to human nature. When oppression comes, human nature fights. It fights for its rights. It fights for release and relief. It demands exoneration and absolution. Sarah's next battle would require that she react to her surroundings with meekness and determination. When everything in her ached to be seen, heard, accepted, and understood, the most powerful weapon she could use was to keep quiet. There would be no self-promotion, no self-preoccupation, no self-preservation, and no self-appointment for Sarah. There would be no self-anything at all. Her unpleasant circumstances dictated that she wait on the only One who could bring light to the situation. He would reveal His plan for her when He chose. She would wait on Him.

Indefinite times of waiting can take the thoughts of a person to places that are never frequented in periods of ease. When humility surfaces and replaces all pride, questions arise that would normally lie dormant. As Sarah waited on the Lord to defend and rescue her in her time of need, she must have wondered about many things. For example, was she really worth defending? What was so special about her that would cause the God of the universe to stop everything He was doing just to help her? Were her needs that important? Would He even want to speak on her behalf after she had lied? Soon she would encounter a love so pure she would know deep down inside that its expression relied on nothing she had done, but solely on the heart of the Giver. In one split second all of the questions would fade away and love would replace the doubt in her heart and mind. She would be defended and experience an unconditional love she never could have imagined, whether in times of difficulty or in times of ease.

Although Sarah was free from captivity and looking forward to her future with her husband and the people she loved, it would take some time to heal from the wounds that had been inflicted by the choices that had been made. She had become a damaged "vessel" requiring the touch of the Master Shipbuilder, Jesus. She would need His touch to move forward. Knowing her need for substantiation, support, and confirmation, the Lord placed it on the heart of the king to publicly announce the error he had made, thus exonerating Sarah. In addition to the public confirmation, the king found it just and right to give Abraham a portion of his wealth on Sarah's behalf. The wounds of the past had begun to heal, and soon she and her story would become an incentive for the weary, joy for those who fought sadness, and words of love for those who hungered for acceptance.

Sarah found herself immobilized when confronted with the roadblock called captivity in her life. Unaware of the Father's plan to rescue her, she did her best to press on. This time of darkness and despair created the perfect environment for the Lord to bring blessings her way. This place of desperation was transformed into a divine delay, a heavenly encounter, and a life lesson designed to transport Sarah closer to the goal and purpose of her life. Inundated with unexpected delights, unanticipated strengths, and unmerited favor, she was given her long-awaited reward. She was given the desire of her heart. She was given her son. Little did she know when it first began that her captivity would be the pathway to her purpose.

Abraham and Sarah had endured the most difficult season of their lives. And in that time of training and testing, they became the people their God desired them to be. They became people of humility. They became people who could be trusted with an eternal legacy. It was their season of darkness that allowed them to desire and seek the light that delivered them from much more than they would ever need to know. As they learned to let go of the past, let go of their agendas, and partner with God and His plan, they were able to grab hold of the future laid out before them. Filled with fruit and the knowledge of the One who made it possible, Abraham and Sarah birthed a nation whose root was their beloved son, Isaac.

Hidden—Not Forgotten

And now it all comes down to you and me and our choices. Will we benefit from the details of this pivotal event in history and take what we have learned and integrate it into our lives? In our confusion, will we let the Lord define who we are and what we are called to be? In our captivity, will we learn how to submit to those in authority over us? In our confinement, will we learn how to serve all people with kindness? In our time of concealment, will we wait on the Lord to reveal our true identity? In our weakness, will we let the Lord defend us? In our worthlessness, will we look to the Lord for validation? In our humiliation, will we look to the Lord for vindication? In our moments of hopelessness and lack, will we let the Lord provide? Will we take the weapons of humility and fight in a way that will ultimately glorify God?

The life of a believer can be difficult at times. And yet when we look to the One who created all things, knows all things, and sustains all things, we are filled with hope and the desire to press on. When we know who we are in Him and release all that we have been, all that we are, and all that we will be, we will find ourselves wrapped in the glorious rhythm of His Spirit. And when times of disappointment and frustration come—and they surely will—you and I will know that just like Sarah and just like the prophet…

We are watching for a sign.

> [Oh, I know, I have been rash to talk out plainly this way to God!] *I will* [in my thinking] *stand upon my post of observation and station myself on the tower or fortress, and will watch to see what He will say within me and what answer I will make* [as His mouthpiece] *to the perplexities of my complaint against Him.*   Habakkuk 2:1

We are waiting for things to change.

> *And the Lord answered me and said, Write the vision and engrave it plainly upon tablets that everyone who passes may* [be able to] *read* [it easily and quickly] *as he hastens by. For the vision is yet for an appointed time and it hastens to end* [fulfillment]; *it will not deceive or disappoint. Though it tarry, wait* [earnestly] *for it, because it will surely come; it will not be behindhand on its appointed day.*   Habakkuk 2:2-3

We are being filled with faith in order for our God to fulfill His plans, purposes, and promises in us and through us.

> *Look at the proud; his soul is not straight or right within him, but the* [rigidly] *just and the* [uncompromis-

ingly] *righteous man shall live by his faith and in his faithfulness.* Habakkuk 2:4

As we wait and watch, we must humble ourselves whole-heartedly and join in the battle the Army of the Lord fights daily for the sake of the harvest. We must surrender to His leadership. We must submit to His training program, considering ourselves as one of many. And we must believe in the Lord's power to carry us through as we step up, step out, and fight.

There is a place for you and me in God's divine plan. He has called us, saved us, and sealed us as His own. Where we find ourselves at the end of today is just the starting point for tomorrow. As we keep our expectations aligned with His, we will reach the goal set before us. Rest assured, my friend, that it is impossible to miss out on His plan unless you have chosen to ignore it completely. And if today you find yourself divinely led into a period of hiding, feel free to expect results above and beyond all you could ask or think. In the Lord's time, He will work in you and through you to make a difference, to leave your mark on those who follow. Be encouraged today, my friend. For a time you may be hidden, but you will never be forgotten.

References

Chapter 1

[1] page 11, *Webster's Ninth New Collegiate Dictionary*
[2] page 17, *Webster's Ninth New Collegiate Dictionary*

Chapter 2

[3] page 19, *Webster's Ninth New Collegiate Dictionary*

Chapter 3

[4] page 36, "Father's Love Letter"

Chapter 4

[5] page 43, *Webster's Ninth New Collegiate Dictionary*

Chapter 8

[6, 7, 8, 9, & 10] page 86, *Webster's Ninth New Collegiate Dictionary*

Chapter 11

[11 & 12] *page 123, Webster's New World Dictionary*

Webster's Ninth New Collegiate Dictionary
Merriam, Webster, Inc. Publishers
Springfield, MA
Copyright, 1990, Principle copyright 1983

"Father's Love Letter," by Barry Adams (by permission, of Father
Heart Communications, copyright 1999-2003)
Douglas B. Wicks, Publisher
Christian Publishing, Inc.
3825 Hartzdale Drive
Camp Hill, PA 17011

Webster's New World Dictionary
Copyright, 1961 and 1966
World Publishing Company
USA